The old East India wharf at London Bridge, ca. 1710. [Peter Monamy p. V. and A. M.]

LIFE AND WORK OF THE PEOPLE OF ENGLAND

A PICTORIAL RECORD *from*
Contemporary Sources

THE EIGHTEENTH CENTURY

BY

DOROTHY HARTLEY

Formerly Art Teacher, The Polytechnic Institute, London

MARGARET M. ELLIOT

B.A., Lond.   St. Aloysius Secondary School, London

G. P. PUTNAM'S SONS
NEW YORK
1931

PREFACE

The object of this series is to give a view of the Social life of each century throug[h] the eyes of the people who lived in it. We have tried to select records suitable for genera[l] and school use. which has meant examining some thousands of MSS., prints, drawing[s] and reference books, and only by careful selection and examination could the result be condensed into an inexpensive series.

A general introduction outlines the characteristics of each century, and a serie[s] of notes gives points of detail. The forty-seven plates comprise about 150 picture[s] covering the main departments of human life.

With the present volume the series is brought to a close, for without a very strongl[y] expressed desire on the part of our readers we shall not attempt the formidable tas[k] of recording the vast activities of the 19th century. In the six volumes we have brief[ly] reviewed life and work from 1000 to 1800 A.D., and illustrated its course with about 1,00[0] pictures. In the 18th century, social life began to take a modern mould, and life generall[y] became more developed, civilised and many-sided. Consequently, in this century mor[e] than any other, we have realised the hopelessness of attempting anything like a repre[-] sentative survey within the limits of our scope. Not only a large volume, but a whol[e] library, could be comfortably devoted to 18th century social life, but at least we hav[e] endeavoured to bring out some of its important salient characteristics—the developmen[t] of industries, beginning to be transformed by the industrial revolution, commerce an[d] trade, the importance of transport, the attention to scientific research and art training, an[d] the large part played by costume, social gatherings, music, and amusements generall[y] Many will no doubt deplore the exclusion of favourite subjects, which could only hav[e] been included by an extension which would have brought this volume right outside th[e] series as planned. It must also be borne in mind that, curiously enough, the 18th centur[y] scarcely seems to have recorded a number of its quite important activities, such a[s] building, medicine and that except by immense research here and on the continen[t] it does not seem possible to get a wide range of examples of such subjects. The exten[t] and variety of English graphic art of the period has enabled us, even more than in th[e] preceding century, to draw our pictures almost exclusively from English sources.

We think it may now be regarded as established that the study of contemporar[y] illustrations is not only desirable and as entertaining as it is instructive, but that [it] is really essential to a right appreciation and well-found understanding of any historic[al] period. It is our wish and hope that this series with all its many defects and still mor[e] numerous limitations will help to this end, both directly and as sign-posts to the great[er] mass of material which is easily available to the appreciative and enquiring student.

Teachers are increasingly enjoying contemporary material directly presented, thoug[h] possibly not as much as their children, to whom it makes an instant appeal, but there [is] room for a wider and deeper recognition of its surpassing interest, and this we believ[e] is sure to come with a general appreciation of the superiority of original sources ov[er] predigested material served up afresh.

Several reviewers and correspondents have suggested the advisability of includin[g] illustrations and descriptions of typical architecture and decoration, etc. We shoul[d] be pleased to comply, but all our available illustration and text space is neede[d] for social life. Building, objects of daily life, etc., really form a separate division. W[e] should enjoy preparing a review of them if there were enough encouragement to hol[d] out hopes of a favourable reception.

The Marylebone Cricket Club has kindly permitted us to include Pl. 13(b) and 40([c]) from their remarkable collection. Mr. Walford of Walford Bros. and Mr. P. Stephenso[n] of G. Rimell & Son have again been invaluable.

As before, we should like to express our deep indebtedness to the authorities of t[he] British Museum. We are also extremely grateful to the Library and Print Room of t[he] Victoria and Albert Museum, the Bodleian Library, Oxford, the Cambridge Librarie[s] and Sir Robert Witt's invaluable and ever-growing collection; and to Mr. Har[ry] Batsford, our publisher, for his unfailing interest and help.

D. R. [
April, 1931   M. M.

MADE AND PRINTED IN GREAT BRITAIN BY THE STANHOPE PRESS LIMITED, ROCHESTER, KENT

INDEX TO TEXT AND PLATES

N.B.—The figures in black type refer in every case to the **plate numbers** of the Illustrations

CONTENTS

SUBJECT NOTE OF PLATES

Some of the sources used for the text of this volume :—

Ladies' Guide, 1700; The Wise and Ingenious Companion, French and English, by Mr. Boyer, 1701; The Present State of Chirurgery, 1703; John Tipper—The Lady's Diary, or the Woman's Almanack, 1703; A Vindication of the Bank of England, by a Merchant, 1707; The Spectator; The Tatler; John Gay—Trivia, or the Art of Walking the Streets of London, 1716; The Weavers' True Case, by a Weaver, London, 1719; The Virtue and Use of Coffee with Regard to the Plague, R. Bradley, 1721; Richard Bradley, A General Treatise of Husbandry and Gardening, 1726; D. Defoe, The Complete English Tradesman, 1726; R. Bradley, The Country Gentleman and Farmer's Monthly Director, 1727; New Principles of Gardening, Batty Langley, 1728; The English Empire in America, Robert Burton, 1728; Richard Bradley, The Gentleman and Farmer's Guide for the Increase and Improvement of Cattle, 1729; Gentleman's Magazine, beg., 1731; Ladies' Magazine; Memoirs of the Life of Barton Booth, Esq., 1733; Calendars of State Papers; Dean Swift, Directions to Servants in General, 1745; The Universal Magazine; An Enquiry into the Causes of the late Increase of Robbers, etc., Henry Fielding, 1751; Z. Conrad von Uffenbach, Merkwürdige Reisen durch Niedersachsen, Holland u. England, 1753; Letters of Richard Radcliffe and John James of Queen's College, Oxford, 1755-83 (Oxford Historical Society, 1888); William Smith, History of the Province of New York, 1757; A Cyclopædia of Arts and Sciences, 2 Vols., 1759; the Complete Sportsman, or, Country Gentleman's Recreation, by Thomas Fairfax, 1760 (?); History of the Travels and Adventures of the Chevalier John Taylor, by himself, 1761; Defoe, A Tour through the Island of Great Britain, 1769; A Complete Body of Planting and Gardening, Rev. William Hanbury, 1770; Arthur Young, "A Six Months' Tour through the North of England," 1770-71; The Complete Servant Maid, Mrs. Anne Barker, 1770 (?); Boswell's Life of Johnson; A New and Universal History, Description and Survey of . . . London and Westminster, by Walter Harrison, 1775; Collections of Virginia Hist. Soc. New Series, Papers (1775-1778) of George Gilmer, M.D., of Albemarle County, V.A.; The Art of English Shooting, by George Edie, 1777; The Complete English Gardener, by Samuel Cooke, 1780 (?); Moritz: Travels through England in 1782; The Works of Sheridan and Goldsmith; Memoirs of G. A. Bellamy, actress, by a Gentleman of Covent Garden Theatre, 1785; Richardson's "Pamela"; A Sentimental Tour through Newcastle, by a Young Lady (Jane Harvey), 1794; Thoughts on Hare and Fox-hunting, Peter Beckford, 1796; The Inoculator or, the Suttonian System of Inoculation, by Daniel Sutton, 1796; Jane Austen's early works; W. H. Pyne, Microcosm, or a Picturesque Delineation of Arts, etc., of Great Britain, 1808; Christopher Anstey, The New Bath Guide, 1809; George Crabbe (1754-1832), Poetical Works; Lives of the Queens of England, Agnes Strickland, 1852; W. H. Calcott, A Few Facts in the Life of Handel, 1859; Macaulay's Essay on Clive, ed. 1877 by H. C. Bowen; John Ashton, Social Life in the Reign of Queen Anne, 1882; Fanny Burney's Diary, ed. 1890-91; A Forgotten Past, F. H. Suckling, 1898; The Lives of the Rakes, E. Beresford Chancellor, 1920; Ambrose Heal, London Tradesman's Cards of the eighteenth century, 1925; Samuel Kelly, the Autobiography of an eighteenth-century seaman, ed. by Crosbie Garstin, 1925; Grove's Dictionary of Music, ed. 1927; Travel Diaries of William Beckford of Fonthill, ed. by Guy Chapman, 1928; Georgian England, by Prof. A. E. Richardson, 1931; Godfrey, The Story of Architecture in England, 1931.

PLATE 2

(a)

(b)

(c)

(d)

(a) A country house kitchen, ca. 1740. [Anon. eng., V. & A. M. Print Room, Port. O 2 C.] (b) Scene in a farmhouse kitchen; the lady is overcome, ca. 1740. [V. & A. M. Print Room.] (c) Instructing little girls in sampler embroidery and lacemaking, ca. 1700. [From a series of plates of trades, V. & A. M. Print Room.] (d) The indignant cook gives a piece of her mind, ca. 1790. [Eng. after T. Stothard, R.A]

LIFE & WORK IN THE EIGHTEENTH CENTURY

INTRODUCTORY NOTE

IT IS impossible to deal in any way thoroughly with the eighteenth century in the short space available ; for it was a period of such enormous change and extraordinary development that volumes could be written without exhausting the subject.

It was also a time of decided transition when much was accomplished, a solid foundation laid. The age was coarse in its manners and to a certain extent brutal in spirit, but the list of great names in all fields of labour and art points to mighty achievements. The age of Anne forms an impressive prelude ; thus early stand the figures of literature, Addison and Steele, Pope and Gay, Swift and Defoe. The beaux of the town, dressed in brocades at £8 the yard, swaggered through the coffee-houses, gambled, drank, and took their snuff in imitation of the gallants of Louis XIV's splendid court ; and their ladies were not far behind them in extravagance.

As the century progresses, other famous names stand out along the way ; statesmen, like Pitt and Burke ; great men of the theatre, Garrick, Goldsmith, Sheridan ; great generals, like Marlborough and Wolfe ; sailors, such as Hawke and Boscawen ; empire-makers like Clive and Warren Hastings ; artists, as Hogarth, Reynolds and Gainsborough ; musicians, beginning with Dr. Arne and the German Handel, who belongs largely to Britain ; religious enthusiasts, such as the Wesley brothers and George Whitefield.

Under the leadership of such men Britain accomplished much. There were of course disastrous wars, as well as successful ones, like the Seven Years' War, so brilliantly carried through to success by the great War Minister, Pitt ; we lost our American colonies, but learnt successful colonisation from that loss ; meanwhile we were firmly rooted in India and Canada, while this expansion and the Industrial Revolution increased our trade.

LANDSCAPE.—The general appearance of English landscape (Pl. 12 (b), 21) shows much alteration during this century. The untidy mediæval stretches of wild country and waste land gradually began to give place to neat enclosed fields and pastures, fit for experiments in revolutionary methods for improving the soil and growing crops. Flocks of plump and prosperous-looking sheep and cattle could be seen grazing after Robert Bakewell and his followers had set themselves seriously to the task of better breeding. Fine, majestic country houses (Pl. 21 (a) (b)) with classical features, telling of an established tradition, rose up on the estates of the wealthy.

But an ominous change was spreading over the country—the migration of country spinners and weavers (Pl. 3 (a), 23 (b)) to the new manufacturing towns built by the invention of machinery. England was becoming a manufacturing country, and smoky chimneys of factories, of spindle and loom began to rise up in favourable districts towards the end of the eighteenth century.

RELIGION.—It is during the eighteenth century that we at last get the beginnings of religious toleration. Though penal laws were still in force against Roman Catholics, who suffered from many restrictions (p. 33) there was now no active persecution.

But the rule of James II had done much to keep alive that absurd fear of Catholicism so long engrained in English hearts.

The general tone of the Church of England was one of toleration—of wide outlook and licence with regard to definite doctrines. One consequence was a coldness and lack of enthusiasm within the English Church ; but zealous preachers came forward in John Wesley (1703-91) and his brother Charles, and George Whitefield (Pl. 39 (d)), who brought the gospel within reach of even the humblest. Excluded from the churches, their powerful open-air sermons made a great impression on the crowds who listened.

Church of England clergymen were for the most part good and worthy men enough, but timid, and often enough the incomes from their livings were pitiably low. A great abuse was the system of "pluralities," by which a clergyman could hold a number of livings and paid a curate a small salary to look after a living.

GOVERNMENT.—Eighteenth century England saw definitely established the rule of a constitutional monarchy, that is, a monarchy under the control of Parliament. When William III came to the throne in 1689 he accepted the crown as a gift from Parliament, under conditions embodied in the Bill of Rights. William saw and accepted this, and it held good henceforth. One attempt only was made to regain absolute authority into the hands of the monarch ; George III, during the earlier part of his reign, tried to dispense with the services of any ministers who would not play into his hands, and therefore did his best to get rid of Pitt ; but his experiment failed.

COUNTRY LIFE AND AGRICULTURE (Pl. 19-21).—During the eighteenth century the rapid growth of commerce and towns drew more country folk to seek their fortunes in the cities. The country landowner in many places resided quietly on his estates, and sometimes, like "Turnip Townshend," devoted himself to the introduction of new methods in agriculture. This was an important step indeed by the wealthier landowner, for smaller farmers could not afford the expense and risk until they saw established results.

One important innovation was the introduction of root-crops. Agriculturalists had been advocating the sowing of turnips, but it was difficult to make the small farmer see the benefit, and not till Turnip Townshend showed the way by growing them largely did the idea really become popular. The turnips were grown in the third field, instead of its being left fallow ; the cattle grazed on these crops, and their manure fertilised the ground for next year's sowing. The turnips also formed winter fodder for the cattle ; formerly much cattle had to be killed off and salted. In this way more people were able to get fresh meat.

Then came Jethro Hull's "drill," a machine for making little ruts in the ground in which the seeds were cast systematically in rows, making it easier to hoe weeds between the rows. In this way, too, there was small chance of wastage, as in the old method of broadcast scattering.

Robert Bakewell, the pioneer of cattle-breeding, bred his sheep (of which the Leicestershires became famous) as much for their good meat as for the wool on their backs, so that their flesh was valuable as well as their fleeces.

TOWN LIFE (see page 28).—In the towns life was busy and exciting. There was keen competition among tradespeople, and trade on the whole flourished. Streets were crowded with pedestrians, coaches (Pl. 7 (a), 22 (a), 24, 33) and sedan-chairs (Pl. 22 (a), 33 (a)), bearing the wealthy to and from the play, the shops (Pl. 24, 25) or card-parties (Pl. 15 (c)). Coffee-houses (Pl. 22 (c)) hummed with life, and amid the smoke of the pipes and the steam from the dishes of coffee, men criticised plans and news, and discussed politics. The fate of many a European Power was decided in the opinions of the coffee-house gallants.

Many old writings and engravings tell us vividly of London life. Here is what Moritz, the German visitor of 1782, says of London (Pl. 24) : "On the left bank o the Thames are delightful terraces, planted with trees, and those new, tasteful buidlings, called the Adelphi. On the Thames itself are countless swarms of little boats (Pl. 34), passing and repassing, many with one mast and one sail, and many with none, in which persons of all ranks are carried over. Thus there is hardly less stir and bustle on this river than London's crowded streets.''

TRADE AND INDUSTRIES.—There was much in eighteenth century life to bring about development and increase of industries ; for example, new inventions and the increased use of certain luxuries. And towards the end of the century came the start of that vast transformation known as the "Industrial Revolution," which was eventually to change England into an industrial nation.

In spinning and weaving (Pl. 28 (a), 29 (c), 30 (b), (c)) Hargreaves' Spinning Jenny, invented about 1764, enabled more than one thread to be spun at a time ; the Flying Shuttle, invented by John Kay, of Bury, enabled weaving to be done faster, and one man to weave cloth of any width by himself. Improvements then came thick and fast, as in Arkwright's machine, and Crompton's "Spinning Mule." The new machines were the wonder of the age. Thomas Newte, in his "Tour in England and Scotland in 1785," tells of Arkwright's two large cotton mills at Crumford, where "the whole process of cleaning, carding, combing, twisting, and completing the yarn for the loom, seemed to be done almost without human aid."

Steam power was used early in the century for mining pumps, like Newcomen's, and later on James Watt showed how useful it could be for mills. And because coal was needed to create steam power, the industries of spinning and weaving tended to drift to the midlands and the north, near the great coalfields.

At Worsley mines, in 1782, Thomas Newte reports that the miners received from 10d. to 3s. a day, according to the quantity of coal dug ; they worked for eight hours. There were usually about 250 tons of coal got in a day, and about 300 persons were regularly employed.

In Staffordshire were the potteries, where Wedgwood was to become famous ; the iron industry flourished at Wilkinson's iron-works in Bersham and elsewhere.

Eighteenth century smiths (Pl. 26 (a)) were kept busy; for not only did they shoe horses (Pl. 26 (d)) and make iron utensils, but they frequently had to manufacture ironwork for houses. Characteristic of Georgian houses are their fine wrought-iron rails, lamps and gates, though later cast-iron came into use.

The increase of and improvement in coaches and sedan-chairs maintained coach-building as an important industry. Carpenters made the coach body, while leather covered the wooden frame, and costly velvets and silks were often used inside. Clockmaking was an important trade, and names like that of Tompion became famous ; English clocks were better than those of other countries.

BUILDING AND ARCHITECTURE.—At the beginning of this century, the style of building had been largely established by Sir Christopher Wren and owed something to Dutch influence (v. "Seventeenth Century," p. 13). Many pleasant little houses were built in town and country, with larger mansions in parks (Pl. 7 (b), 21 (a), (b)). They were usually square in plan, of mellowed brick, or stone in districts like the Cotswolds, with classic door, sash windows, and central pediment. The interior had usually fine wood panelling, with a spiral turned-baluster stair. The more important houses have ceiling paintings. There are nice lead rainwater heads and iron-work gates ; the original formal gardens (Pl. 21 (b)) have probably gone. As examples, see No. 44 Great Ormond Street, London ; Maid-of-honour Row, Richmond ; and Compesson House, Salisbury Close.

About 1720 a school of architects rose who ignored Wren and considered Inigo Jones their master ; everything had to follow the principles of the Italian architect Palladio, so that the age to 1760 is often called Palladian. Houses were more often of stone—colder and more classic, with plaster panelling, classic motives in the ceiling and Renaissance chimney-pieces (Pl. 14 (c)), often in two stages. The same stairs persisted, though we also get ironwork balustrades. Bath is full of good Georgian houses, and the great Norfolk houses of Houghton and Holkham have rich craftsmanship. Look also at the Horse Guards and Admiralty, London. But many interiors show the florid plaster twistings of the Rococo style, often by wandering Italians (see St. Martin's-in-the-Fields). There are also found Chinese forms, the result of a great attraction for the Far East. Georgian churches (Pl. 24, 39 (a)) were often erected; do not despise them, like rabid Gothicists; they are usually worthy, comfortable places, with much good detail and better practically and artistically than the spiky churches of the Gothic revival. Robert Adam and his brothers introduced a lighter style in decoration, with late Roman and Pompeian motifs, and painted roundels. They favoured curved rooms ; 20 St. James Square is a splendid town house ; and you can see their typical work at Kenwood. Lastly, from 1790 to 1820-30 comes the Greek revival, often called Regency, when everything became severe and restrained, with literal Greek forms, especially in the honeysuckle or anthemion ornament. Houses were usually stucco-covered, like the pleasant terraces of Brighton, with curved bay windows, and the villas of Clifton and Cheltenham. Sir John Soane carried out many original designs. Even at this last stage of the Renaissance we get little touches of refinement—fanlights, cast-iron gates, or trellis balconies, and some well-designed shop fronts.

GARDENS.—At the beginning of the century gardens were entirely formal (Pl. 21 (b)), as shown in Kip's engravings of 1720 and thereabouts. They were influenced by the Dutch, and the French style of Le Nôtre, and though bitterly abused later, they had much dignity and architectural character. We find in them terraces, pastures (geometrical lay-outs of beds), forecourts and many other charming features, such as statues, iron gates, great avenues, cut hedges (Pl. 6 (b)), mazes, and topiary, or trees cut into fantastic shapes, afterwards hugely ridiculed by the wits. Beautiful examples are found at Drayton, Northants and Levens, Westmorland.

About 1730-40 a very different type of lay-out called landscape gardening was first devised by William Kent. The gardens at Stowe (Pl. 7 (b), 17 (a)) are typical. With wide vistas, groves of trees and classical temples and monuments, this variety is reminiscent more, perhaps, of a stretching landscape than a garden; the style was long popular on the Continent as "le jardin anglais." Under the pretentious "Capability" Bown much beautiful old work was swept away for a bare effect of dotted clumps, endlessly twisting drives, and lakes with winding streams, often artificially engineered.

DECORATION AND FURNITURE.—It is impossible to give a full account of the furniture and other decorative crafts through all of their manifestations of Late Stuart, Chippendale, Hepplewhite, Sheraton and English Classic styles. But the decorative work of the eighteenth century is usually of refined design and excellent craftsmanship, and it is to be hoped that you will learn to appreciate it and study the treasures which form part of our artistic heritage in wood-carving, silver and plate, iron and brass, porcelain and earthenware, enamel, glass, textiles, carpets embroidery and even printed stuffs. The Victoria and Albert Museum, South Kensington, is a great treasure-house for those who live in or can visit London, but a selection of eighteenth century art is usually to be found in local museums of important towns.

DOMESTIC LIFE (Pl. 41 (c)).—We have diaries and memoirs (see p. 28) that give interesting details of home life. Institutions like clubs and coffee-houses (Pl. 22 (c)) meant more social life for men, and in London the gardens of Vauxhall and Ranelagh (Pl. 4 (d)) provided concerts (Pl. 4 (a), 15 (e), 17 (a)) and suppers for the wealthier folk ; Bath, Tunbridge Wells and other watering-places had crowds of fashionable patrons.

The townsman could take his meals at an eating-house. Moritz records his impressions of one ; he went there with friends, and, "we paid a shilling each for some roast meat and a salad, giving, at the same time, nearly half as much to the waiter ; and yet this is reckoned a cheap house."

But country folk, particularly during the winter, were isolated on account of bad roads, and thrown very much on their own resources.

Except in the higher circles, life was not formal. The greater households had their bands of servants, and the mistress organised and supervised their labours. The number of eighteenth century cookery books reveals the variety and amount eaten (see page 28). Beer and ale were still drinks for the common folk, and wine for the richer, though tea, coffee, and chocolate were now fashionable. "I would always advise those who drink coffee in England," writes Moritz, "to mention beforehand how many cups are to be made with half an ounce ; or the people will probably bring them a prodigious quantity of brown water."

AMUSEMENTS (Pl. 12-18).—Among country gentlemen we find hunting (Pl. 12) and racing popular. They hunted the stag, hare and fox. Books on sport abound at the end of the eighteenth century. Fox-hunting was only for the upper classes ; always a gentlemanly sport, it seems to have been the chief occupation for a country gentleman, and George III set the example himself. Game Laws, inflicting grievous penalties on all not of the privileged class, were severely enforced, and gave rise to great numbers of poachers.

Horse-racing (Pl. 12 (a)) had steadily increased since the Restoration, when Charles II had shown delight in the pastime. Important races were held at Epsom, Newmarket, Ascot (Pl. 12 (a)) and Doncaster. For ball-games there were football, skittles (Pl. 13 (a)) bowls, golf and cricket (Pl. 13 (b), (c)) (in which ladies took occasional part) ; boxing became increasingly popular. Rough and cruel sports like bull- and bear-baiting and cock-fighting still flourished. Old rural games and jollities were kept up on occasions like fairs (Pl. 16). Every district had at least one annual fair, which brought thousands together, and was a great time for merriment and wild behaviour.

The town beaux for the most part patronised more "genteel" amusements than their country prototypes. They had routs and balls (Pl. 4 (d), (e)), pleasure-gardens (Pl. 4 (d)), concerts (4(a), 15 (e), 17 (a)) and card-parties (Pl. 15 (c)). Gambling was very popular with both sexes, and huge sums were lost and won over loo and whist.

The eighteenth century beaux and ladies were great playgoers. Covent Garden, Drury Lane and the Haymarket Theatres flourished (see page 25) and we have a number of great actors and actresses : e.g., Garrick, Mrs. Siddons, Mrs. Clive, Peg Woffington.

COSTUME (Pl. 4-6, 22, 32).—Generally speaking, English fashions were copied from France, though towards the end of the period English modes were original in men's costume.

Men wore full-skirted coats (Pl. 18 (b), 39 (b)) shaped to the waist, with stiffened-out skirts ; the coat reached to the knees, and the vest or waistcoat (Pl. 5 (d), 18 (b)) was nearly as long. After 1750, however, the stiffened-out, full-skirted coats began to go out of fashion, and by degrees men's coats were adapted into the "cutaway" style with a high waist (Pl. 2 (b), 10 (c), 40 (c), 42 (b), (d)) ; and the waistcoat became shorter. At first, when waistcoats were long, the knee-breeches were hardly seen, but, as the century wore on, became more visible with the shorter waistcoat. Breeches were fastened at the knees with buttons and a buckle, or sometimes ribbons. Fashionable stockings often had clocks, and the usual footgear consisted of shoes with big square buckles (Pl. 5 (d)), though high boots (Pl. 10 (c)) were worn by riders, and later on when walking.

The typical eighteenth century gentleman's hat was the familiar "three-cornered" type (Pl. 2 (d)) ; variety was shown in the prominence of the three points and the angle at which it was worn. Later we can see the beginnings of the "top-hat," with a high crown and a less prominent brim (Pl. 5 (c)). Wigs were an important item. The voluminous full-bottomed wig (Pl. 5 (d), 10 (a)) was still in vogue till about 1750, when we find the tendency to draw the hair back and tie it in a "queue."

Here is a description of a foppish young man who came to visit an eighteenth century actress, as found in her memoirs. "He had on a white surtout, with a crimson cape, a Parisian waistcoat, his hair en papillate, a feather in his hat, a couteau de chasse by his side, a small cane hanging by his button, and two Italian greyhounds."

An eighteenth century lady's costume (Pl. 2, 4-6) consisted generally of a pointed bodice fitting the figure, with elbow or long sleeves, a skirt reaching at least to the ankles, and very full on the hips. At first the hooped petticoat came into its own again, and gradually it was worn standing out stiffly only at the sides (Pl. 4) as in the typical "Polly Peachum" costume. For riding (Pl. 5 (c)) and hunting ladies wore modified masculine coats, and for ordinary outdoor wear they had various styles of cloaks.

Fashionable ladies powdered their hair, but at first hairdressing was fairly simple, with a few curls at the sides and the rest drawn back. By degrees hair-dressing modes became more elaborate and artificial (Pl. 4 (e)). The hair was padded with cotton wool to make it stand up higher, and some false hair was often worn. More and more absurd it became, till the head looked an enormous erection, be-decked with ribbons, feathers, little toy ships, and coaches. Later, little caps of lace were worn indoors, and a mode came in for "milkmaid" straw hats tied under the chin in imitation of Marie Antoinette, Queen of France. Innumerable varieties of hat were introduced (Pl. 4, 5), profusely decorated with fruit and flowers ; the head was the most conspicuous and highly ornamented part of a modish lady's appearance.

Shoes were high-heeled early in the century; later on a little lower; they were often of brocade, ornamented with ribbons or buckles. The court lady was besides encumbered with such accessories as fans, long gloves, muffs, parasol, flowers, arti-ficial or otherwise ; and dare not appear without her complexion powdered and patched. Face patches must have been dear to the English lady, according to Misson, the Frenchman who wrote his impressions of the English early in the century. He says : "The use of patches is not unknown to the French ladies ; but she that wears them must be young and handsome. In England young, old, handsome, ugly, all are bepatched till they are bed-rid. I have often counted fifteen patches or more upon the swarthy wrinkled phiz of an old hag three-score and ten and upwards."

The end of the century saw a remarkable change. Dresses were long, full but skimpy, and clinging to the figure (Pl. 5 (c), 42 (b)); to get this effect the dress was sometimes worn damp! The waist rose up to immediately under the arms, the gown was low-necked. This style was known as "classical," and to correspond the Greek mode of hairdressing was adopted, with a low "classical" sandal.

LITERATURE.—The eighteenth century was a golden age for literature. Often the writer had a hard fight ; he was on the whole badly paid, but a talented author usually managed to make himself recognised, for although the reading public was small, its taste was discriminating. The journal formed a considerable part of ordinary reading, and such papers as "The Spectator" and "The Tatler," begun by Richard Steele and Joseph Addison under Anne, helped to spread a certain culture among the coffee-house habitués.

Daniel Defoe was a journalist-author who handled a variety of subjects. He left us an interesting "Journal of the Plague Year," accounts of tours round the country, and in 1719 published the ever-popular "Robinson Crusoe," a story of adventure that set the fashion for scores of imitators. Dean Swift wrote bitingly sarcastic comments on the life of his time, of which "Gulliver's Travels" is the chief.

Alexander Pope was the leading poet of this early period. His witty and learned verses in such works as "The Rape of the Lock" and "The Dunciad" brought him fame and profit. Later we have the beginnings of romantic poetry in Thomas Gray, whose "Elegy in a Country Churchyard" is said to have inspired General Wolfe with such admiring envy.

The fame of Dr. Samuel Johnson rests rather upon his capabilities as a critic and his brilliant conversation than upon his actual writings. Johnson became the accepted and admired literary critic. As an author he is chiefly known for his "Dictionary" and "Lives of the Poets." We have a remarkable account of his life from the pen of his biographer, Boswell.

The eighteenth century saw the birth of the English novel. Samuel Richardson wrote "Pamela" (v. illustrations by Highmore, Pl. 6 (c), 33 (c), 39 (b), 41 (c)), telling the story by means of letters, and followed it up with "Clarissa Harlowe." Other well-known novel writers are Lawrence Sterne, who wrote "Tristram Shandy" and the "Sentimental Journey," and Fielding, author of "Tom Jones," and Smollett. Dr. Johnson was of opinion that "there was more knowledge of the heart in one letter of Richardson's than in all 'Tom Jones.' "

Johnson was acquainted with other well-known figures of his time. Among them may be mentioned Oliver Goldsmith, the Irish writer who wrote "The Vicar of Wakefield," and one of the most famous plays, "She Stoops to Conquer." Richard Sheridan was the author of the brilliant comedies, "The Rivals," the "School for Scandal" and "The Critic."

MUSIC (Pl. 4 (a), 15 (e), 16 (a), (b), 17).—There were not many English composers of note, but musical taste became well developed and good music made a wide appeal. The German Handel settled and wrote his best music here ; and English musicians like Dr. Arne, Arnodl, Jackson and Linley, did good work and were appreciated. Johann Christian Bach, youngest son of the great Sebastian, became court musician after Handel, and Haydn and Mozart visited England. The Hanoverian royal family were very musical. Queen Charlotte, wife of George III, had been taught by one of the Bach's, and accompanied by Mozart. George III was passionately fond of music and played the organ.

There is the romantic story of Thomas Britton, the famous musical "small-coal" man, who after setting up in business for himself after his apprenticeship to a dealer in small-coal, instituted a concert in a room over his coal-house ; to which, though the house was small and the stairs steep, audiences comprising quite "polite" people were attracted.

For the lower classes, the violin (Pl. 4 (a), 15 (e), 17 (a)), sometimes contemptuously known as the "fiddle," was perhaps the most popular and handy instrument ; it was in constant use at country festivities. But people were learning to appreciate the strings in good music. Well-known Italian violinists in London were besieged with demands for lessons, and gave concerts at the great houses. There were harps (Pl. 15 (e)), and flutes (Pl. 15 (e), 17 (a)), organs, cellos (Pl. 4 (a), 17 (a), (c)), bassoons and oboes ; the harpsichord (Pl. 15 (e), 17 (b)) and its successor, the pianoforte. In the harpsichord sound was produced by quills that plucked the wire strings. As time went on the number of strings to each key was increased, and this gave a fuller tone to the note. Last came the full development of the piano, and late in the century we have the first great English piano, the Broadwood.

The "fugue" type of music was much favoured, with various "voices," each with a melody, and all answering each other. It was only later that composers began to use one melody, with the other parts to harmonise and accompany it. Then there were gay little dance suites (Pl. 14 (d)), minuets and sarabands and gigues, and popular songs. A very striking and beautiful collection, largely traditional, was made in Gay's "Beggar's Opera" (Pl. 18 (b)), first produced in 1728, and recently revived. These joyous little melodies are genuinely English, and very fascinating in their tuneful simplicity.

ART.—The first prominent English painter was William Hogarth (see for example Pl. 18 (b)). At first he earned his living by designing engraved plates for tradesmen, but painting fascinated him, and he took it up as a career. Hogarth has depicted e.g., in "The Rake's Progress" and "Marriage à la Mode," grim and cruel, but realistic, scenes from daily life.

Then after an interval come the great portrait painters. Sir Joshua Reynolds became a prominent "man about town" besides a famous artist ; he was for long the most fashionable painter, and made portraits of nearly all important persons. He was able to demand high fees and to live in sumptuous style. George Romney travelled in Paris and Rome and it was only as a middle-aged man that he settled down to paint portraits. Among his many noteworthy sitters was Emma Hart, afterwards Lady Hamilton.

A third name must be mentioned, Thomas Gainsborough. Very early he showed signs of great talent, particularly for landscape drawing. He studied at St. Martin's Lane Academy, and before he was twenty he was earning good sums. After an early marriage Gainsborough settled in Bath, and for fifteen years he was busy with portraits of the fashionable persons who visited the town. Later, he moved to London and won even greater fame.

There are many others whose names find a place in the sphere of English eighteenth century art. Thomas Rowlandson (Pl. 26 (d, e), 34 (d)) stands out as in some sense a successor to Hogarth, though his style was more delicate. He studied in Paris, and devoted himself to brilliant drawings satirising English life.

George Morland's talent is best shown in his pictures of country life. He loved an irregular existence, and though this did not tend to better his circumstances, it gave his rural scenes value and accuracy. Then there was William Blake, who lived a quiet, retired life, a painter and poet in one, till well into the nineteenth century. His work was not appreciated during his lifetime, as it was entirely unsuited to the period.

Other names of this time are : Opie, Sir Thomas Lawrence, Raeburn, Ibbetson, West, Joseph Wright of Derby, and Zoffany, a foreigner who became prominent in eighteenth century painting. Francis Wheatley was among the best known of those who popularised the circulation of coloured prints ; Wheatley's series of the "Cries of London" is extremely well known.

To the end of the century belong Crome, Cotman, Girtin (who died young) and, above all, John Constable, the great landscape painter ; the latter belongs mainly to the next century.

Sculpture in England was chiefly in the hands of foreigners during the early eighteenth century. Roubilliac, the most brilliant, made statues that served as models for English potters. But a number of English sculptors were doing moderately good work. However, it was in the reign of George III that sculpture began seriously to come into its own, and John Flaxman is famous as a really great sculptor of the later period. Flaxman made designs for the great potter, Wedgwood, and studied in Rome. Later, he made statues of famous personages like Warren Hastings and Lord Howe, with many monuments.

In 1768 the Royal Academy of Arts in London was founded, with Sir Joshua Reynolds as its first President. Its object was to "cultivate and improve the arts of painting, sculpture and architecture," and it established schools for art students. Gainsborough was one of its earliest members.

TRAVEL AND TRANSPORT (Pl. 32-35), (see page 27).—Travel was frequent, but the state of eighteenth century roads certainly did not encourage it. There were few roads worth the name ; most were impassable in bad weather. The agriculturist Arthur Young, in his journey from Newport Pagnel to Bedford, wrote in 1770 : " . . . if I may venture to call such a cursed string of hills and holes by the name of road ; a causeway is here and there thrown up, but so high, and so very narrow, that it was at the peril of our necks we passed a wagon with a civil and careful driver." And, travelling from Grimsthorpe to Colsterworth in Lincolnshire, he went eight miles along a track "called by the courtesy of the neighbourhood a turnpike"; but along this turnpike, he says, "we were every moment either buried in quagmires of mud or racked to dislocation over pieces of rock which they term 'mending.' " But our German friend Moritz travelled to Oxford and found "a charming, fine broad road." Perhaps that was in comparison with those of his native land !

The increasing use of coaches (Pl. 7 (a), 22 (a), 24, 33) and large wagons (Pl. 32 (a) made ruts in the roads, and the wheels of many a vehicle stuck fast. Hence, pack-horses (Pl. 32 (b), 34 (e)) were frequently used for the transport of goods in many districts. But in the course of the century attempts were made to deal with this problem. The system adopted, however, was to suit the traffic to the roads. The use of wide wheels was encouraged, because it was thought that they would not make such dangerous ruts. The "turnpike" system became widespread— at intervals along the roads were toll-gates, whose keepers demanded from travellers a certain sum towards the upkeep of the road they were using. People resented this turnpike system fiercely, but it held its ground, and at least kept public attention alive. But it was not until the nineteenth century, when Macadam first produced a good method of road-making, that English roads were at all notably improved.

All who could afford it kept a private coach ; and for passengers who wanted cheap fares and had no objection to a slow journey many wagon services were run for passengers and goods. The mails were generally carried by riders, or by rather slow, small vehicles ; but in 1784 special fast coaches began to take them, and this gave a special impetus to road-improving, for the stopping of mails was a serious business.

Public stage-coaches ran between all the more important towns. Moritz liked his experience in one English stage-coach. He writes : "I had the luxury of being driven in an English stage. These coaches are, at least in the eyes of a foreigner, quite elegant, lined in the inside, and with two seats large enough to accommodate six persons ; but it must be owned, when the carriage is full, the company are rather crowded. . . Persons to whom it is not convenient to pay a full price . . . sit on top of the coach, without any seats, or even a rail . . . you constantly see numbers seated there and in perfect safety . . . these people only pay half as much as those inside." But once he travelled outside to Northampton, and was terrified out of his life ; he tried to get relief by climbing into the luggage basket, but got so battered and shaken that he had to get back to the top.

A great hindrance to enjoyable travel was the highwayman. Numbers infested the roads, and Captain Macheath of the "Beggar's Opera" must have been a familiar figure. In spite of very severe penalties the number of highwaymen did not seem to lessen, and they went to their deaths with a gallant bearing that impressed the immense crowds who watched the scene.

The eighteenth century is the canal century (Pl. 34 (d), 35 (b)). Defoe, writing early in the century, remarks on the lack of waterways and the need for horse-traffic (Pl. 32) ; "The English," he says, "have a great deal of business for horses, and that almost in all parts of the island ; they have but little inland navigation, and therefore not only their husbandry requires the labour to their cattle, but most part of the heavy goods, which are carried from place to place, in trade, are carried by land."

It was discovered that artificial waterways, connecting natural ones on which towns were built, would reduce the cost of transport. The Duke of Bridgewater, with the talented engineer Brindley, spent much money and thought on schemes. A canal was made connecting the duke's mines at Worsley with Manchester ; and when coal could be brought by barge (Pl. 34 (a), (b), (d)) instead of in baskets on pack-horses, it lowered the price by 50 per cent. Then came Brindley's Manchester Ship Canal, and soon there arose a great network of waterways.

LAW AND PUNISHMENTS (Pl. 10).—The punishments for offenders were dreadful in their severity. For the smallest thefts a man or woman was hanged (Pl. 10 (b)), and a woman, Catherine Hayes, who in conjunction with a man called Billings murdered her husband, was burned at the stake.

During the eighteenth century the dreadful state of English prisons (Pl. 10 (a), (d)) was exposed through the devoted work of Oglethorpe and John Howard (see page 31). Howard, after his investigations of prison life, published accounts of what he had seen. Prisons were crowded out, there was insufficient food, and the prisoners were herded together, really bad criminals with first offenders or those wrongly accused. Jailers were cruel and merciless, demanding money to treat their prisoners properly. Sanitary conditions were appalling ; there was seldom enough fresh air, and many prisoners died of "gaol fever," a mysterious illness prevalent in prisons. Worst of all, a man could be detained awaiting trial sometimes as long as a year. Debtors were imprisoned indefinitely till they could pay or some good friend helped them. It is pleasant to read in a book of memoirs, that a certain Lord Digby used to visit the Marshalsea Debtors' Prison at least twice a year, pay the debts of a number of prisoners, and give them money till they could find work.

Howard advocated such reforms as better sites for prisons with a view to better water supply, better food, and worthier jailers. To him and Oglethorpe belongs the credit of first rousing the nation against these evils, and they caused improved conditions in many prisons.

Executions (Pl. 10 (b)) were public sights, and drew large crowds. Here is a sailor's account of one he witnessed :

"Hearing on board that several people were to be hung at Tyburn the next day, I agreed to accompany several of our seamen to see the execution. Therefore the next morning we got to Newgate some time before the prisoners were ready to leave the prison. We kept close to the door, round which a large concourse of people had assembled. We waited to see the prisoners put into the carts, and then made the best of our way to Tyburn (passing St. Sepulchre's Church, where the passing-bell was sounding its discordant notes in the ears of the poor criminals). We got near the gallows, in the midst of such an assembly of people as I have never witnessed before, nor never wish to see again on such an occasion. The malefactors consisted of a Jew, five or six other men, and one woman, . . a servant, who let her sweetheart rob the house of plate. He was also hung by her side."

A most profitable way of infringing the law was by smuggling (see page 32). Most goods coming from abroad had to pay customs duty ; in some coastal districts it was comparatively easy to land foreign goods, like tobacco, tea and wines, far from any customs house, and distribute them by means of loaded pack-horses (Pl. 34 (e)). Officials were appointed to keep a sharp look-out, but many people were able to make a living by this practice. Adam Smith, writing his "Wealth of Nations" in 1776, created a stir by questioning the advisability of levying these duties, and advocating free trade. But it was not until the middle of the nineteenth century, by which time the number of dutiable articles had been minimised and more efficient patrolling introduced, that smuggling died a natural death.

CHILDREN AND EDUCATION (Pl. 40-42).—Very young children were first taught their letters by means of horn-books—sheets of stiff paper, with the letters of the alphabet and the vowels written on them, placed under a cover of thin horn, with a wooden handle to hold it by. The horn enabled the book to withstand the wear and tear of child usage.

There were many boarding schools for both girls and boys (see page 26, 27). Boys were educated chiefly with a knowledge of the classics—to the detriment of their knowledge of English, some writers declared. In one number of "The Spectator," early in the century, there is a complaint that schoolboys, "when they are got into Latin are looked upon as above English, the reading of which is wholly neglected, or at least read to very little purpose." Moritz gives an account of one "seminary of learning." "Of these places of learning, here called academies," he says, "there is a prodigious number in London and its vicinity ; though, not withstanding their pompous names, they are in reality nothing more than small schools, set up by private persons. Dr. G. keeps an academy for the education of twelve young people, which number is never exceeded, and the same plan has been followed by many others." Dr. G. had a large board over the door with "Dr. G.'s Academy" on it. The schoolroom was furnished with benches, and a professor's chair or pulpit. The usher, a young clergyman, seated at a desk, taught boys Greek and Latin grammar ; the boys declined Latin in "the old jog-trot way." At this school "before and after dinner the Lord's Prayer was repeated in French ; after dinner, the boys had leave to play in a very small yard. . . Mr. G. himself instructs the children in writing, arithmetic, and French, all which seemed to be well-taught ; especially writing, in which the young people in England far surpass, I believe, all others."

The young lady of prosperous parents was trained to be accomplished, to increase her chances of winning a suitable husband. One "town young lady" writes that her father, a tradesman, sent her to boarding school, where she learnt to dance and sing, play on various instruments, paint on glass, make sweetmeats and sauces, and "everything that was genteel and fashionable."

The eighteenth century was not a particularly flourishing period for the two universities. Such earnest students as Dr. Johnson were not too common ; he, unfortunately, was obliged on account of poverty to leave Oxford before taking his degree. We read of one student at Queen's College, Oxford who refused to take a studentship at Christchurch : "They were all either stupid or dissipated," he writes. "I learnt nothing, I played at tennis once or twice, I took to reading Greek of my own fancy, but there was no encouragement ; we just went to the foolish lectures of our tutors, to be taught something of logical jargon."

MEDICINE AND SCIENCE (Pl. 43, 44).—It can hardly be said that eighteenth century medical knowledge was of a high standard. There was no doubt a percentage of good doctors, but it was pre-eminently an age of quacks. The credulous public would believe anything if expressed in high-sounding terms ; quack ointments, pills, and tonics were widely sold and did considerable harm. Poor sanitary arrangements, and frequently insufficient or unhealthy water supply, with over-eating and drinking, must also have caused many premature deaths.

Rough operations were still performed by barbers and apothecaries ; a writer of 1703, commenting on "the present state of chirurgery," remarks of a particular locality, "Scarce one who does not bleed, cut issues, treat apostems, apply plaisters, pultisses and fomentations. The great numbers of punctured tendons and arterys, stiff and useless joynts, etc., are lasting examples with how much judgement they have performed the first."

But the same writer declares that "the Art of chirurgery is at this time in a more flourishing state than ever" ; and that the city of London can produce a greater number of men, eminent in that profession, than any other in the world.

In this century inoculation against smallpox and other virulent diseases began to be practised. Smallpox was rampant till inoculation became current. One Richard Radcliffe writes of his inoculation in 1767. He was put on strict diet ; and after the operation he seems to have suffered little beyond a slight headache. He was soon allowed "to eat and drink and live as I pleased ; and after paying the doctor five guineas, and expending about four pounds upon other occasions, I returned to Colsterworth (Lincolnshire) the Tuesday following." He states that seventy people were inoculated in that parish by a common country apothecary ; but all recovered, and none suffered anything worth speaking of. Other instances were far less favourable.

John Abernethy is the best-known British surgeon. Born in 1764, he studied medicine at St. Bartholomew's and London hospitals (Pl. 44 (a)). He became assistant surgeon at the latter and later principal surgeon. He used to give lectures to students at his own house, but such great crowds attended that they could not all be accommodated, and the hospital authorities built a lecture theatre. This gifted surgeon was notorious for his gruff manner and the short shrift he gave self-pitying patients. Abernethy died in 1831.

Scientific research continued to be increasingly encouraged by the Royal Society, the oldest scientific society, which had begun during the Restoration. In 1703 the great Sir Isaac Newton became its president till his death in 1727. The society continued to increase in importance, among other things taking over the direction of the Royal Observatory at Greenwich. Throughout its history the Royal Society has frequently been consulted by the Government on scientific matters. The most famous name in chemistry is that of Joseph Priestley (see p. 34).

LAND WARFARE (Pl. 45, 47).—The history of British warfare in this century is remarkable for the careers of some great soldiers. Early in the period we have the Duke of Marlborough, brilliant campaigner against the ambitions of Louis XIV. His genius and ability as a commander-in-chief are most striking.

The struggle between English and French in Canada afforded opportunities for great soldiers like Wolfe and Cornwallis, Clinton and Burgoyne. Of these, Wolfe stands out. As a very young man his great talent was recognised, and at twenty-three he was already a lieutenant-colonel. He was masterly in his brilliantly daring exploits, as in his final achievement, the scaling of the Heights of Abraham at Quebec in 1759. "My way," replied Wolfe once to some one who recommended the motto 'slow and sure,' "is 'quick and sure.' That is the best way."

In India, the genius of Robert Clive was able to use native quarrels to help the British East India Company, and by his campaigns he definitely gained an ascendancy over the French.

Towards the end of the century came the rise of Wellington, and the history of British warfare culminates in the Napoleonic Wars, ending with the Battle of Waterloo in 1815.

It was not a simple matter to raise the fighting forces necessary. A certain number of criminals was recruited for the army, and debtors were often enlisted from prison. All sorts of methods were used by the recruiting sergeants to enrol those "at a loose end," Life was not easy for the recruit, and army conditions abroad were very bad ; there was often little sympathy between officers and men.

The chief weapon of Marlborough's and Wellington's men was an improved form of the "fire-lock" gun (Pl. 45 (a), (b)). In the Napoleonic Wars the English "Brown Bess" was noted—a flint-lock musket with a short brown barrel. During these wars English gunmakers made their work superior to that of foreign manufacturers. Joseph Manton was the most famous of English gunsmiths.

SEA-FIGHTING AND SHIPS (Pl. 35-38, 46).—The great achievements of the British Navy of the eighteenth century are remarkable when we consider the difficulties that had to be overcome. The naval victories must be greatly attributed to the splendid ability and fine spirit of the English sailor, rather than to the vessels them-

PLATE 3

(a)

(b)

(c)

(a) Various ways of spinning and winding, c. 1750. [Diderot, " Encyclopædia."]
(b) A typical tailor's shop, London, 1749. [Boitard dr., Bickham eng.] (c) Beating
carpets at Oxford, 1772. [Oxford Almanack, E. and M. Rooker dr. & eng.]

lves and the organisation and discipline. Life on board was often very hard for the
ilor, though it had its attractions in the constant adventure and the chance of
nsiderable prize-money. There were brutal floggings for punishment, in some cases
flicted with cruelty, though no doubt this has been exaggerated.

The sailors' food was often very bad. Samuel Kelly, a sailor on the *Grenville*,
eclares the provisions there to have been "of infamous quality." "The beef," he
ys, "appeared coarse, and such as is cured for negroes ; the barrels of pork con-
sted of pigs' heads, with iron rings in the nose, pigs' feet and pigs' tails with much
air thereon. Each man had six pounds of bread and five pounds of salted meat per
eek, but neither beer, spirits, nor candle were allowed." But about the middle of
ie century Admiral Vernon introduced the ration of rum-and-water. The equip-
ent for ships' doctors and surgeons was very poor, and this niggardliness was the
use of many deaths and failure to heal wounds.

A number of men were obtained for the navy by the "press-gang" system com-
on in the century, (p. 36) and many criminals preferred the navy to prison when
ven the choice. Dockyards (Pl. 36 (a), (b), (d), 37 (c), 38 (c)) were improved,
ıd steam machines began to be used in shipbuilding at the end of the century.

Among the great naval commanders of the century were Benbow, Byng, Anson,
empenfeldt, Jervis, and finally Lord Nelson.

THE EXPANSION OF THE BRITISH EMPIRE.—This age is noticeable for the growth
British empire beyond the seas. In North America the rivalry between French
ıd British settlers resolved itself into a great struggle that ended in the acquisition
Canada by Britain, and the domination of English-speaking peoples in North
merica. The loss of the thirteen States by the War of American Independence,
ough it detracted from British power, left a British-born people in control, and we
ill kept Canada. In India, Clive turned the activity of a trading company into the
undation-stone of British rule over a vast country inhabited by varied races.
aptain Cook, the naval explorer sent by the Admiralty in 1768 to search for the
ntinent supposed to exist in the South Pacific, reached New Zealand. For six
onths he explored the coasts ; then he reached "New Holland," or Australia, and
amined the east coast, naming one district New South Wales because of its appa-
nt likeness to Glamorganshire.

Looking back on eighteenth century England, we cannot but be impressed with
r achievements and progress. There was a certain brutality and coarseness in
anners, with much culture among the upper classes. The penal laws make us
udder with their glaring lack of humanity, and they never diminished the number
criminals. But at the same time there was an increasing respect for law and
der, an appreciation of individual rights, a genuine if exaggerated patriotism, a
iblic conscience aroused against abuses like the bad prison system and the slave
ıde. It was no small sign of progress, too, that the standard of living was raised
r all classes, and prosperity became more generally diffused. An increase in trade
d commercial development followed as a natural result of the expansion of the
itish Empire. Eighteenth century England more than held her own among other
tions, and the champions of political freedom and personal independence looked
English government as their model.

AGRICULTURE

YIELD OF WHEAT.—A well-known agriculturist has given us a comparative view the fertility of the various counties of England. He makes the usual produce of whe per acre in Lincoln and Rutland, which stand highest, to be 28 bushels ; Northumberlar 27, Sussex 26, Leicester and Stafford 25, Devon and Essex 24½, Berks, Derby, Ker Lancaster, Middlesex, Norfolk, Northampton, Somerset, Warwick and Worcester 2 Cambridge 23½, Chester, Hertford and Surrey 23, Dorset and Hereford 22½, Cumberlan Hants, Nottingham, Suffolk, Wilts and York 22, Buckingham 21½, Durham 21, Bedfor Cornwall, Monmouth, Oxford, Salop and Westmorland 20, Gloucester 18, and Huntin don 15.

THE THRESHING MACHINE.—The flail is effectual, but the labour is severe, and tl operation tedious. The first threshing machine was invented in Edinburgh, by Micha Menzies, about 1732. It consisted of a number of instruments like flails, fixed in a mo able beam. The second was the invention of Michael Stirling, Dumblane, Perthshire. third threshing-mill was invented in 1772 by two persons in Northumberland, near about the same time and on the same principles. Andrew Meikle, of Tyningham, Ea Lothian, completely succeeded in 1785 ; and afterwards obtained a patent.

CIDER.—"In cider-making the apples are kept stored up till they begin to swe They are put into a mill and ground into a kind of wet powder, if we may use the expre sion. This is put into hair bags and squeezed in a press. The juice falls into a vessel a is then tunned. After a proper time, families, or the cider-dealers, bottle it ; for exce in the cider counties, it is generally drunk from the bottle, not from the cask.

"After the juice, which forms the strong cider, is expressed, water is applied to the d residuum of apples. In thirty-six hours, or thereabouts, there is produced a small cid for the kitchen, which they call ciderkin."

The foregoing extracts from C. Gray in W. H. Pyne's "Microcosm," 1806.

HAY HARVEST.—

Now swarms the village o'er the jovial mead ;
The rustic youth, brown with meridian toil,
Healthful and strong ; full as the summer rose,
Blown by prevailing suns, the ruddy maid,
Half-naked, swelling on the sight, and all
Her kindled graces burning o'er her cheek.
E'en stopping age is here ; and infant hands
Trail the long rake, or, with the fragrant load
O'ercharg'd amid the kind oppression roll.
Wide flies the tedded grain ; all in a row,

Advancing broad, or wheeling round the field,
They spread their breathing harvest to the su
That throws refreshful round a rural smell ;
Or, as they rake the GREEN-appearing ground
And drive the dusky wave along the mead,
The russet hay-cock rises thick behind,
In order gay. While heard from dale to dale,
Waking the breeze, resounds the blended voic
Of happy labour, love and social glee.
(Thomson's "Seasons

SPORTS, AMUSEMENTS, THE THEATRE, MUSIC

CRICKET.—"Cricket, when played in high style, exhibits a most pleasing and animati spectacle. Of this we have proofs every week during summer in Lord's far-celebrat cricket-ground. The players are generally dressed in white or nankeen. Some excel batting, and exhibit uncommon quickness of eye in ascertaining whether the ball com in such a direct line with the wicket, as to require blocking, or so oblique as that th may strike with safety. Some are noted for bowling slow and slyly ; others for bowli strong. There are bowlers that send the ball with incredible force ; it seems like cannon-shot. Some make excellent short-stops, and others as good long ones. T fieldmen have their various qualifications, too ; some for acting near, and some at distance. A skilful director knows the forte of each of his men, and places him accordingly

RACING SPEEDS.—"A few anecdotes of the speed and exertions of racehorses w not be out of place. Hambletonian and Diamond, in the celebrated race between the at Newmarket, ran the Beacon course of 4 miles in 8 minutes and 20 seconds. Rapid this is, it is by no means extraordinary. In 1763 the Marquis of Rockingham's B Malton, at York, ran 4 miles in 7 minutes and 43¾ s."—C. Gray, in W. H. Pyne's "Micr cosm," 1806.

COCK-FIGHTING.—Hogarth has left us an engraving of a typical cock-fight. It w certainly a most barbarous sport. Every town had its cockpit, where these birds, ca fully trained and trimmed and fitted with little steel spurs, were set on to attack ea other, amid wild excitement and betting from the spectators. Conrad von Uffenbach

German who wrote the story of his travels in England and other countries in 1753, seems to have been very impressed with the extraordinary keenness with which the English enjoyed cock-fighting. When there is to be a cock-fight, he says, printed leaflets are circulated announcing the fact, and in the newspapers lovers of the sport are told of the cocks that are fighting, the wagers laid on their victory, etc. "The people, whether of high or low rank," he remarks, "behave like madmen, betting higher and higher, up to 20 or more guineas."

A THEATRE AUDIENCE IN 1782.—Moritz' experience at the Haymarket is amusing and worth quoting. "For a seat in the boxes you pay 5s., in the pit 3s., in the first gallery 2s., and in the second or upper gallery, 1s. And it is the tenants in this upper gallery who, for their shilling, make all that noise and uproar, for which the English play-houses are so famous. I was in the pit, which gradually rises, amphitheatre-wise from the orchestra, and is furnished with benches, one above the other, from the top to the bottom. Often and often, whilst I sat here, did a rotten orange, or pieces of the peel of an orange, fly past me, or past some of my neighbours, and once one of them actually hit my hat, without my daring to look round, for fear another might come plump into my face.

"Besides this perpetual pelting from the gallery, which renders an English play-house so uncomfortable, there is no end to their calling out, and knocking with their sticks, till the curtain is drawn up. . . I sometimes heard, too, the people in the lower or middle gallery quarrelling with those of the upper one. Behind me, in the pit, sat a young fop, who, in order to display his costly stone buckles with the utmost brilliancy, continually put his foot on my bench, sometimes upon my coat ; which I could avoid only by sparing him as much space, from my portion of the seat, as would make him a footstool.

"In the boxes, quite in a corner, sat several servants, who were said to be placed there to keep the seats for the families they served, till they should arrive ; they seemed to sit remarkably still and close, the reason of which, I was told, was their apprehension of being pelted ; for if one of them dares but to look out of the box, he is immediately saluted with a shower of orange-peel from the gallery."

"*March* 5, 1737.—A vast number of footmen assembled with offensive weapons, broke open the doors of Drury Lane Theatre, and fought their way to the stage-door, which they forced open, and prevented the reading of the proclamation by Colonel de Veil. He caused several of the ringleaders to be taken and committed to Newgate, many were wounded in the fray, and the audience much terrified, among whom were the prince and princess of Wales. The pretence for this disturbance was, that the footmen were locked out of the upper gallery, which they claimed as a privilege."—"*The Universal Chronologist,*" II.

MUSIC.—As far as composers are concerned, Dr. Arne stands out prominently ; he wrote music after the style of Italian opera, but we know him best for his settings of Shakespeare songs, and the famous "Rule, Britannia."

One ought perhaps to mention the writers of the tuneful melodies to Sheridan's one opera, "The Duenna," the two Thomas Linleys, father and son. It is worth while to note that our National Anthem, "God Save the King," was first publicly recognised when Dr. Arne played the accompaniment to it amid scenes of great enthusiasm, at Drury Lane Theatre in 1745. A young lady, Jane Harvey, writes in her 'Sentimental Tour through Newcastle," in 1794 : "After supper, the parson, who is a capital performer on the German Flute, entertained us with several favourite airs—and in particular the favourite and charming one of 'God Save the King.' "

George Frederick Handel first settled in London in 1710. His first opera, "Rinaldo," was performed in 1711, but it was his grand oratorios, of which the chief is the "Messiah," that raised him so high among the musicians of his time. Handel became the teacher of music to the children of the Prince of Wales under George I. He won the king's favour by the "Water-music," composed for the Royal Family's river journey by barge. Handel, however, incurred much expense in the production of his works in London ; he went to Dublin, and here the "Messiah" was produced, having been written in twenty-three days.

"*May* 1, 1753.—The sacred oratorio of the Messiah was performed at the chapel belonging to the Foundling-hospital, under the direction of Mr. Handel ; on which occasion, there were about 800 coaches and chairs ; the price of the tickets amounting to 925 guineas."

"*May* 26, 1784.—A jubilee took place in Westminster Abbey, in commemoration of Handel, when 600 performers were employed ; the profits amounting to 12,746 l."

"*June*, 1786.—A musical festival, consisting of 640 musicians, was performed in commemoration of the great Handel."—"*The Universal Chronologist*," II.

> "Some say, compared to Bononcini,
> That Mynheer Handel's but a ninny ;
> Others aver, that he to Handel
> Is scarcely fit to hold a candle ;
> Strange all this difference should be
> 'Twixt Tweedledum and Tweedledee."

—Dean Swift's epigram on the squabbles between Handel and Bononcini on the directorate of the Opera Company, when the sopranos Faustina and Cuzzoni came to blows.

"On a new overture being played in Crow-Street Theatre (Dublin), Mr. D——, as he was squinting through his glass from the manager's box, very sagaciously observed that the horns did not play ; irritated at this supposed neglect he flew to the door of the box which leads behind the scenes, and enquired of Hitchcock, the poor pitiful prompter what was the reason the horns did not play ? He immediately ran to Giordani, who presided on this occasion at the harpsichord, and repeated his master's inquiry ; the other desired the inquisitive prompter not to trouble himself about the business ; for that the horns, in such a part of the overture, had a rest. 'A rest !' rejoined the sensible manager, when the embassy was delivered, 'then, Sir, I insist on the horns being forfeited; for, damn me, if any man shall have the least rest in my theatre.'"(*An Answer to Memoirs of Mrs. Billington, written by a Gentleman, etc.*, 1792.)

CHILDREN AND EDUCATION

"A child is no sooner born than it is bound up almost as firmly as an Egyptian mummy in folds of linen . . . in vain for him to give signs of distress . . . the old witch who presides over his infant days winds him up in his destined confinement. When he comes to be dressed like a man he has ligatures applied to his arms and legs and middle to prevent the circulation of his blood. If it be of tender sex, she must be bound yet more straightly about waist and stomach."—*A Contemporary Review*.

"Parents scourge your Children that are subject to lying, for it is a Fault not to be suffered."

To Children.—"In the Morning, after you have got up and dressed yourself, and fiinshed your Duty to God (that is your Prayers), then wash yourself, comb your Hair and do all those things that are usual for you to do, before you go down Stairs ; then go down, when you see your Parents bow to them, after you have bowed to them enquire after their Health, in these or the like Words,—how do you do, Sir ? or, Papa I hope you are well ? I hope you have had a good Night's Repose. In the same Manner you must salute your Mamma.

"When you receive Orders to go into the Room where your Parents are, bow, stand still till such Time they bid you sit down, or inform you what is their Pleasure with you . . . sit still, upright, and silent ; look not at any one that is in the Room, . . . so as to stare or ogle at them . . . play not with anything about you viz., Buttons, Handkerchief and the like ; put not your Fingers in your Mouth, bite not your Nails, make no Faces . . . make no Noise with your Feet . . . put not your Hands in your Pockets ; turn your Toes out, lay not one Leg over the other."

"If you cannot avoid sneezing or coughing, turn aside and make as little Noise in doing it as you possibly can ; it is very vulgar in any one to make a Noise in coughing and sneezing."

"You should have a special care not to make any Kind of Faces ; that is, such as grinning, winking, or putting out your Tongue, and the like ; for that will make you despised."—*The Young Gentleman and Lady's Private Tutor*. By Matthew Towle (Dancing Master in Oxford). 1770.

"Academies.—Young Gentlemen are instructed in the various branches of English and French, including Washing, Book-keeping, Algebra and Mathematics, and the Use of the Globes. Thirty pounds per annum.

"N.B.—Young Gentlemen wearing light trousers, etc., the washing will be 10s. per year extra."

"To instruct the youthful mind in moral and religious principles forms an essential part of the rules of this seminary."—*Contemporary Trade Card*.

"Terms of Mrs. Masquerier's Boarding School, Upper End of Church Lane, Kensington. Board, including French, English, Writing, Arithmetic, Geography, Needlework and Dancing, for Twenty Guineas a Year and One Guinea Entrance. Parents or Guardians may depend on the utmost care taken of the Young Ladies' morals and manners and a particular tenderness shewn to their persons. N.B.—The house is genteel and the situation remarkably beautiful. To those who do not chuse to learn all the above branches a reasonable deduction will be made. A shilling stage to Holborn, Wood Street, and the Bank, several times a Day."—*Trade Card*, 1782, B.M.

TRAVEL AND TRANSPORT

THE STATE OF THE ROADS.—"Before the establishment of turnpikes on the road to Poole, in Dorsetshire, such was its plight, that in order to go from a gentleman's seat not six miles off to that port for coals, the waggoner used to get up early in the morning, and it was often late at night ere he got home again. In winter sometimes the waggon stuck fast, and both men and horses could not get it on.

' A gentleman of Hertfordshire, who, like other leading gentlemen formerly, kept a set of six horses, used, with these, forty or fifty years ago, to take two days to get to London. This journey was only about thirty miles, but it was in November, and the body of the coach often rested on the road. He used to join also his team of oxen to the regular set of six horses.

"In the year 1754 a *flying coach* was advertised; and the advertisement stated that *however incredible it might appear, it would certainly arrive in London in four days and a half after leaving Manchester.* This is now (1800) in thirty hours, and has been done in less.

"About fifty years ago (1750) a clergyman jogging slowly along on a horse that served both for ploughing and riding, to the general assembly of the church of Scotland at Edinburgh, saw two horses tied to a gate and the London mail on the saddle of one of them. Coming up he looked over to learn what had become of the riders. He there observed two lads playing at penny stones, or quoits. Holding up his whip, *You rascal,* said he to the one nearest him, *how dare you leave the mail thus exposed on the public road? O, Sir,* cried the boy in great alarm, *it's not me. That's the postboy there: I am only an express.*"

"WAGGONS.—The mode of carrying on our internal commerce by means of large waggons, in which so considerable a capital is now employed, is but of modern date. Anciently the intercourse was but trifling, as well as very irregular; and the goods were conveyed on the backs of horses. The wheels of these great waggons, from their convexity, and being covered with rings of iron, look clumsy when seen on the road. Were they made flat, or nearly so, the weight on them would press equally on all parts, and the friction would be diminished. They would then be rather an advantage to the roads, as they would smooth and consolidate. But, constructed as they are, when the materials of the highway have been loosened, they are more apt to operate like a plough than a roller.

"CANALS.—The inland navigation of Great Britain has within half a century increased to an astonishing extent both on rivers and canals but particularly in the latter. Many of these have amply repaid the speculators. Some have proved unprofitable but perhaps in time those at present unproductive may yield a handsome profit."—*The above from C. Gray in W. H. Pyne's "Microcosm,"* 1806.

Moritz had rather a bad time at inns. People were very rude to him indeed; once, at Nuneham, five miles from Oxford, they banged the door in his face. But the people at the inn in Oxford showed Moritz why he had been so rudely received on his journey; they said that those who went on foot for so long a journey were looked upon in the same light as beggars, but added that the farther he got from London the more reasonable and humble should he find the people; "everything would be cheaper, and everybody more hospitable." In an inn at Windsor Moritz had to share a room with another man, who came in noisily just as he was going off to sleep, and stumbled against Moritz's bed. When he found his own bed, he threw himself on it without pulling off clothes or boots.—*C. P. Moritz "Travels Through England,"* 1782.

TOWN LIFE—HOUSEHOLD AND DRESS—HOUSES AND GARDENS

STREETS AND SIGNS.—Moritz speaks of the "admirable manner in which the streets are lighted up"; and says, "the footway, paved with large stones on both sides of the streets, appears, to a foreigner, exceedingly convenient and pleasant." Of the shops Moritz remarks that every person of every trade "makes parade with a sign at his door"; there is hardly a cobbler whose name, etc., may not be read in large golden letters. "Children educated here," "Shoes mended here," "Foreign spiritous liquors sold here" and such notices, can be read on many doors.—*Moritz, Tour*, 1782.

TRADE DISTRICTS.—"In most towns, but particularly in the City of London, there are places as it were appropriated to particular trades, and where the trades which are placed there succeed very well, but would do very ill any where else, or any other trades in the same places; . . . as the booksellers in St. Paul's Churchyard, about the Exchange, Temple and the Strand, etc., the mercers on both sides Ludgate, in Roundcourt, and Gracechurch and Lombard-streets; the shoemakers in St. Martins le Grand, and Shoe-maker-Row; the coachmakers in Long-acre, Queen Street, and Bishopsgate; butchers in Eastcheap, and such like."—*Defoe, "The Complete English Tradesman,"* 1726.

COFFEE HOUSES.—Misson says: "These Houses, which are very numerous in London, are extremely convenient. You have all Manner of News there: You have a good Fire, which you may sit by as long as you please; You have a Dish of Coffee, you meet your Friends for the Transaction of Business and all for a Penny, if you don't care to spend more."

STREET SNARES.—

"Seek not from Prentices to learn the Way,   Let not the Ballad-singer's thrilling Strain
Those fabling Boys will turn thy steps astray.   Amid the swarm thy listening Ear detain;
Ask the grave Tradesman to direct thee right,   Guard well thy pocket; for these syrens stand
He ne'er deceives, but when he profits by 't.   To aid the Labours of the diving Hand."
       —*John Gay, "Trivia or The Art of Walking the Streets of London,"* 1719.

HOUSEHOLD AND DRESS

MEALS.—"There are some Noblemen that have both French and English Cooks, and these eat much after the French manner; but among the middling sort of People they have 10 or 12 sorts of common meats, which infallibly take their Turns at their Tables, and two Dishes are their Dinners; a Pudding, for instance, and a Piece of Roast Beef; another time they will have a piece of Boil'd Beef, and then they salt it some Days before hand, and besiege it with 5 or 6 Heaps of Cabbage, Carrots, Turnips or some other Herbs or Roots, well pepper'd and salted, and swimming in Butter; a Leg of Roast or Boil'd Mutton, dished up with the same Dainties, Fowls, Pigs, Ox Tripes, and Tongues, Rabbits, Pigeons, all well moistened with Butter, without Larding; Two of these Dishes, always serv'd up one after the other, make the usual Dinner of a substantial Gentleman, or wealthy Citizen. When they have boil'd Meat, there is sometimes one of the Company that will have the Broth; this is a kind of soup with a little Oatmeal in it, and some Leaves of Thyme or Sage, or other such small Herbs. They bring up this in as many Porringers as there are People that desire it; those that please, crumble a little Bread into it, and this makes a kind of Potage."—*Henri Misson. "Travels through England."*

October 28th, 1717.—Bill of Fare at a Company dinner—(small one).

"3 dishes of boyled Fowles and Bacon, with Oyster Sauce (2 in a dish)—2 Turkeys and Chines—2 Marrow Puddings—3 galls. red and 1 gall. white wine—Beer, bread, apples—lemons, sugar etc."

Servants and Dishwashers paid on this occasion 2 shillings.

HAIRDRESSING, ETC. FOR LADIES—Hair; either bright, black or brown, not thin but full and waving, if it falls in *moderate* curls the better, but black is particularly useful in setting off the whiteness of neck and skin.

Eyes black, chestnut or blue.

Eyebrows—well divided, rather full than thin, semi-circular and broader in the middle than the ends.

Cheeks should have a degree of Plumpness.

Mouth small.

Chin white, soft and agreeably rounded.

Neck white, straight, soft and flexible ; long rather than short, less above and increasing gently towards the shoulders, the whiteness and delicacy of its skin should improve to the Bosom, till shoulders white and gently spread.

The Hands should unite insensibly with the arms and be long and delicate.

The Bosom white and charming, the breasts of equal roundness, whiteness and firmness.

The sides long, Hips wider than Shoulders, Knees rounded, legs straight and the feet finely turned, white and little.—"*The Ladies Guide,*" 1700.

There were several types of queue. Sometimes the back hair of the wig was fastened into a black bag ; or it might be plaited, in one or two or even three plaits, or "clubbed," i.e., tied in the middle of the queue. Then came such innovations as side-pieces of hair punched out over the ears, or roll curls. Those who wore wigs had their own hair cropped close to the head, but some gentlemen preferred to powder and arrange their hair in imitation of a peruke.

COSTUME.—A List (or Inventory) of the Habits of an English Lady.

A Smock of Cambrick Holland, about 3 ells and a half at 12s. per ell ..	2	2	0
Marseilles quilted Petticoat, 3 yards wide and a yard long	3	6	0
Hoop-Petticoat covered with Tabby	2	15	0
French or Italian Silk quilted Petticoat, 1¼ yard deep, and 6 yards wide	10	0	0
Mantua and Petticoat of French Brocade, 26 yards, at £3 per yard ..	78	0	0
French Point or Flanders Lac'd Head, Ruffles and Tucker	80	0	0
Stays covered with Tabby (English)	3	0	0
A French Necklace	1	5	0
Flanders laced Handkerchief	10	0	0
French or Italian Flowers for the Hair	2	0	0
Italian Fan	5	0	0
Silk Stockings, English	1	0	0
Shoes, English	2	10	0
A Girdle, French		15	0
A Cambrick Pocket Handkerchief		10	0
French Kid Gloves		2	6
A black French silk Alamode Hood		15	0
A black French Lac'd Hood	5	5	0
Imbroidered Knot and Bosom Knot, French	2	2	0
	£210	**7**	**6**

From a Contemporary Book of Tracts, B.M.

HOSE.—"The calves of these stockings are thickened a little too much ; they make my legs like a porter's . . . let the next be the thickness of a crown piece less. . . remember, Mr. Hosier, that if you make a nobleman's Spring legs as robust as his Autumnal calves, you commit a monstrous impropriety."

" . . . And the shoe is of no earthly use, but to keep on the buckle."—*Sheridan, "A Trip to Scarborough."*

HOUSES AND GARDENS

THE £500 A YEAR HOUSE.—"Barton Cottage though small was comfortable and compact . . . the building was regular, the roof was tiled, the window shutters were *not* painted green nor were the walls covered with honeysuckles (as a cottage). A small green court was the whole of its demesne in front, and a neat wicket gate admitted into it. . . A narrow passage led directly through the house into the garden behind. On each side of the entrance was a sitting room about 16 ft. square and beyond . . . were the offices and the stairs. Four bedrooms and 2 garrets formed the rest of the house. . . till these alterations could be made from the savings of £500 a year by a woman who never saved in her life. . ."—"*Sense and Sensibility.*" *Jane Austen, November,* 1796-1798.

GARDENS.—"Gardening is at this time so esteemed by almost everyone, that scarce a person from the peer to the cottager thinks himself tolerably happy without being possessed of a garden . . . the gardener's task is become easy by the nursery man doing the greatest part of it for him."—"*The Gardener's Notebook,*" 1779.

"There are few remains now of the old grotesque style of gardening, in which the trees were cut into shape of birds, beasts, buildings and so forth. This style, which appears so ridiculous and laughable to us, was no doubt thought extremely fine by our ancestors. In the meantime, we are adopting and applauding fashions, which our successors will think as grotesque, and laugh as heartily at, as we do at those of our predecessors. Genuine nature alone pleases forever."—*C. Gray in W. H. Pyne's "Microcosm,"* 1803.

INDUSTRIES, TRADE AND ART

"A LOOM AND THROWSTER'S MILL (Pl. 29 (c), 28 (a)).—The woof thread is wound on little tubes of paper or rushes so disposed that they may easily be put in the shuttle. The warp thread is bound on large wooden bobbins to dispose it for warping and when warped (i.e., set up in the loom frame) it is stiffened with size (that made from shreds of parchment is the best).

"At the loom are two workers 'which throw transversely the shuttle one to other' (or single-handed looms made narrower cloth). 'The cloth is taken off the loom, cleared of knots, ends . . . and other filth . . . with little iron nippers.'

"The cloth is then 'pulled,' dressed with potter's clay, water and afterward soap suds (the soap most esteemed is the white, of Genoa); this pulling process is done under heavy mallets in troughs. It is then washed and combed over by teazles and cleaned several times till fine.

"The cloth thus wove, scoor'd, and shorne is sent to the dyer and afterwards pressed to a smooth finish with a slight gloss. In France, none but scarlet, green, blue, etc., receive this last preparation, blacks being judged better without it.

"The Loom needs no explanation; the Throwster will fill the bobbins from the skeins of wool, the Horse and boy below provide the winding force, on the floor above a woman waits to catch and knot together any thread that breaks in the winding."—*"An Encyclopædia of Arts and Sciences,"* 2 v., 1759.

GLASS WORKING (Pl. 29, b).—On the left are glass blowers spinning or twirling out the glass into their disks which can be cut and used for ordinary purposes (this is the early uneven bottle glass window lights, see Vol. fifteenth century), the right side shows a tank of molten glass being lifted from the furnace and poured out upon the level table top. Instantly the man at the end will roll his roller across to spread it flat and the piece of plate glass is wheeled away to cool.

Behind a man is shown breaking up the 'frit' glass conveniently for the cistern. Glass is then ground and polished by hand with pads and emery and tripoli stone. 'The most admirable operation in the grinding way is the grinding of optic glasses. This has always been a skilled and tedious job.'—*"An Encyclopædia of Arts and Sciences,"* 2 v. 1759.

"CHARCOAL BURNERS.—In making charcoal, the wood is split or cut into pieces two or three feet long, and placed on the ground endwise, inclining towards a centre. The stack is covered with turf, and the surface plastered with a mixture of earth and charcoal dust well tempered together. It is kept burning, with a few vents opened, till it is completely charred, which is known by the appearance of the smoke. All apertures are then closed up, with a mixture of earth and charcoal dust, which by excluding the external air, prevents the coals from being any farther consumed, and the fire goes out of itself. The operation generally requires two days and a half if the wood be dry, but if green fully three days."—*C. Gray in W. H. Pyne's "Microcosm,"* 1806.

"TRADE.—In 1710 the setting up of a Pastry-Cook's shop cost upwards of £300. *Outfit:* (1) Sash windows, all of looking-glass plates, 12 ins. by 16 ins. in measure. (2) All walls of shop lin'd up with galley tiles—and the Backshop with galley tiles in panels, finely painted in forest-work and figures. (3) 2 large Pier looking-glasses and one chimney glass in the shop, and one very large Pier glass 7 foot high in the Backshop. (4) 2 large branches of Candlesticks, one in the shop and one in the back-room. (5) 3 great glass lanthorns in the shop, and 8 small ones. (6) 26 sconces against the wall, with a large pair of silver standing candlesticks in the back-room, value £25. (7) 6 fine large silver salvers to serve sweetmeats. (8) 12 large high stands of rings, whereof 3 silver, to place small dishes for tarts, jellies, etc., at a feast. (9) Painting the ceiling, and gilding the lanthorns, the sashes, and the carved work £55. Small plate, china basins, cups, etc. Building 2 ovens about £25. £20 in stock for pies, cheese-cakes, etc. "

Defoe thinks it absurdly extravagant and quite unnecessary.—Defoe, *"The Complete English Tradesman,"* 1727,

"Edw. Nourse, Mercer, at ye Turks-Head, near Bow-Church, Cheapside, London, Sells all Sorts of Genoa, Dutch and English Velvets Paduasoys of all Colours, Tabbys water'd or unwater'd. Rich Brocades, Damasks and all Sorts of Flower'd Silks, Rich Florence and English Sattins, Figur'd and Stript Lutestrings, Ducapes. Mantuas, Sarsnets and Persians, Likewise all Sorts of half Silks as English and Turkey Burdets, Cherry-derrys figur'd and Stript Donjars. Also all Sorts of Black Silks for Hoods and Scarves, Worsted Damasks. Plodds, Superfine broad Camblets, Calimancoes, Camblitees, Black Russels, fine Callimancoes for Pettycoats and Yard wide Tamnys or Stuffs. Likewise Short Cloaks, Manteels. Mantelets and Velvet Hoods, ready made, with all other sorts of Mercery Goods, Wholesale and Retail at ye lowest Prices."—*Trade Card, ca.* 1735.

ART AND DECORATION.—Hogarth's six pictures, representing the Marriage a-la-mode, were purchased for 1000 l. by Mr. Angerstein (1797)" (whose collection later formed the nucleus of the National Gallery).—*"The Universal Chronologist,"* II.

"T. Sheraton, 106 Wardour Street, Soho, 1795. Teaches Perspective, Architecture and Ornaments. Makes designs for cabinet makers and sells all kinds of drawing books." —*Trade Card.* (The celebrated Furniture Designer ; died at No. 8 Broad Street, Golden Square, 1806).

"T. Sandby, Junr., St. Georges Row, Oxford Street, Terms of teaching Drawing.

> One Scholar, Eight Lessons, Two Guineas.
>
> Two Do.   Three Do.
> Three Do.   Four Do.
> Four Do.   Six Do."—*Trade Card, about* 1770.

"At the Maiden-head in Bow-church-Yard. London. Shop Keepers Bills are Curiously Engrav'd on Copper Plates. By Wm. and Cluer Dicey. Likewise All manner of Business Printed with the greatest Expedition at the Lowest Rates."—*Trade Card, about* 1750.

"John Brown, at the Three Cover'd Chairs and Walnut Tree, the East Side of St. Paul's Church Yard, near the School. London. Makes and sells all sorts of the best and most fashionable Chairs, either Cover'd, Matted, or Can'd. Likewise all Sorts of Cabinet Work, with sconces, Pier and Chimney Glasses, Mohogany and other Tables : Blinds for Windows made and Curiously Painted on Canvas, Silk or Wire : Where is good Choice etc., best painted of any in London, none excepted. N.B. Upholsters work of all sorts neat and cheap."—*Trade Card, about* 1750.

LAW AND PUNISHMENT

STATE OF PRISONS.—*"February* 18, 1729.—A member of the house of commons (James Oglethorpe, Esq.) having a friend in the Fleet prison, named Castel, an ingenious artist, whom he used to visit, on being informed that the hardships Castel suffered in that prison had occasioned his death, moved, that a committee might be appointed to inquire into the state of the gaols of this kingdom ; which, being carried into execution, Mr. Oglethorpe was made chairman. They then visited the Fleet prison on the 27th February, and examined several of the prisoners, and among the rest Sir William Rich, Bart., whom they found loaded with heavy irons by the warden, Mr. Bambridge, upon which they ordered his fetters to be taken off ; but the committee found him the next day. The house of commons, in consequence, ordered Thomas Bambridge, Esq., to be taken into custody by the serjeant at arms.

"March 28, 1746.—The lord mayor ordered Ventilators, invented by the Rev. Dr. Hales, to be fixed in several apartments in Newgate to let in wholesome air."— *"The Universal Chronologist,"* II.

STREET ROBBERS.—

> "Though thou art tempted by the Link-man's Call
> Yet trust him not along the lonely Wall ;
> In the Midway he'll quench the flaming brand,
> And share the booty with the pilfering Band."

The Pillory.—
> "Where elevated o'er the gaping Crowd,
> Clasp'd in the Board the perjured Head is bow'd,
> Betimes retreat ; here, thick as Hailstones pour,
> Turnips, and half-hatched Eggs (a mingled Show'r)
> Among the rabble rain ; some random throw
> May with the trickling Yolk thy Cheek o'erflow."—
> *John Gay, "Trivia."*

"*Wednesday*, 20*th April*, 1768. Turlis, the Common Hangman, was much hurt and bruised by the mob throwing stones at the execution of three malefactors at Kingston."

"*Monday*, 6*th March*, 1769. On Friday, a tradesman, convicted of wilful and corrupt perjury, stood in and upon the Pillory in High Street, Southwark, and was severely treated by the populace. They also pelted Turlis, the executioner, with stones and brickbats, which cut him in the Head and Face in a terrible manner."—*Two extracts from the "Public Advertiser."*

Smuggling.—"*February* 20, 1751. A hearse drawn by four horses, the driver being in a black cloak, was stopped by two officers, assisted by soldiers, a mile from Shoreham, in Sussex, wherein was discovered a large coffin, covered with black, containing a great quantity of gold and silver, French laces, cambrics, and a parcel of tea, all of which were sent to the Custom-house, at Shoreham."

"*August* 1, 1778. Tea and coffee were seized in the Fleet prison to a very large amount, which had been conveyed over the walls with the assistance of the prisoners, who had received warehouse rent for the same."

"*June* 1, 1778. Three hundred pounds were awarded as a verdict against three officers of the customs, for seizing articles which were not contraband goods."—*The Universal Chronologist," II.*

SHIPPING

Hark the Boatswain hoarsely bawling,
By topsail-sheets and haul-yards stand ;
Down top-gallants be quick hauling
Down your stay-sails, hand, boys, hand ;
  Now it freshens—set the braces,
The top-sail sheets—now let go ;
  Loof, boys, loof ! don't make wry faces ;
  Up your top-sails nimbly clew.

Now top-sail yards point to the wind, boys ;
See all is clear to reef each course.
Let the foresheets go—don't mind, boys,
Though the weather should grow worse.
  Fore and aft the sprint sail yard get ;
Reef the mizzen, see all clear
  Hands up, each prevents brace set ;
  Man the foreyards, cheer, lads, cheer.

—The foremast's gone—cries every tongue out
O'er the sea, twelve feet above deck ;
A leak beneath the chestrels sprung out ;
Call all hands to clear the wreck.
  Quick the lanyards cut to pieces ;

Come, my hearts, be stout and bold.
  Plumb the well—the leak increases—
  Four feet water in the hold !

(While o'er the seas wild waves are beating,
We for wives and children mourn.
Alas ! to them there's no retreating ;
Alas ! to them there's no return.)
  Still the leak is gaining on us ;
Both chain pumps are choked below
  (Heaven then have mercy on us !
  Only that can save us now).

O'er the lee beam is the land, boys ;
Let the guns o'er board be thrown.
To the pumps come every hand, boys ;
See, her mizzen mast is gone !
The leak we've found ! it lessens fast
We've lightened her a foot or more ;
Up and rig our Jury Fore-mast,
  She rights—she rights ;
    We're off Shore !
      —*"The Tempest,"* 1700.

"That the great wages which are given in the merchant service, and the very low wages in her Majesty's, is one occasion that men do not readily enter themselves therein : therefore it is proposed that the merchant's wages be lowered to 30s. per month, so that none by any fraudulent or collusive ways give more ; and that the pay of the seamen in her Majesty's service be raised to 26s. per month to the able sailors before the mast, and 21s. per month to quarter gunners."—*Sir John Norris, Vice-Admiral of the Blue Squadron of her Majesty's Fleet* (1704). *Brit. Mus. Addl. MS.* 28134.

William Lem, Broker, Sells Ships or parts of Ships by Publick or Private Sale. Lets Ships to Freight, Enters and Clears Ships at the Custom House : Makes Insurances on Ships and Merchandise. Attends at his Office in Exchange Alley, London, from 9

the Morning till 8 in the Evening. ORDERS left at his House in Lime Street, or at his
ffice, will be punctually complyd with.

SHIP-MASTERS—The Henry and ffrancis. Robert Osborn Master is now loading at
he Custom House Key.

AGENT IN NAVAL AFFAIRS: MOTTO, Let us Bang the Dons. Transacts Officers,
eaman and Mariner's Business or for their relations.—*Various Trade Cards*.

CHURCH AFFAIRS

"*May* 11, 1776. It was determined by the court of king's-bench, that the want of
parsonage-house should be no excuse for the non-residence of a clergyman."

"*April* 3, 1790. A clergyman at Leicester Assizes, for marrying a couple without
ther publication of bans, or a license, was sentenced to fourteen years' transportation."

"*March* 23, 1790. A Jewess, at her own sole expense, caused a synagogue to be
rected in Broad-court, Leadenhall Street."

"*May* 12, 1718. The English Government, having been informed that the papists
ere going to celebrate the feast of St. Winifred, at Holywell, in Wales, sent down a
arty of dragoons who seized their priest as he was officiating, with the image, plate,
nd other utensils, and found papers which contained the settlement of many estates
o superstitious uses."

"*Oct*. 12, 1743. This day, being the anniversary of Edward the Confessor's birth,
great number of Roman Catholics were prevented from paying their devotions at his
hrine as usual, orders having been given that the tombs in Westminster Abbey should
ot be shewn on that day."—*"The Universal Chronologist," Part II*.

"The rain and hail drove through our coats—great and small—boots, and every-
hing, and yet froze as it fell, even upon our eyebrows, so that we had scarce strength
n motion left when we got to our inn at Stilton" (on the Great North Road).—*John
Wesley on a northern journey, early in* 1747.

"One evening, Mr. Wesley stopped his horse to pick the blackberries, saying,
Brother Nelson, we ought to be thankful that blackberries are plentiful, for this is the
est country I ever saw for getting an appetite, but the worst that I ever saw for getting
ood'."—*John Nelson, Wesley's follower, on their journeys in Cornwall*.

"Long rides, miry roads, sharp weather! Cold houses to sit in, with very moderate
uel, and three or four children roaring or rocking about you; coarse food, and meagre
quor; lumpy beds to lie on, and too short for the feet; stiff blankets, like boards, for
covering; rise at five in the morning to preach; at seven, breakfast on tea, made
ith dirty water; at eight, mount a horse, with boots never cleaned, and then ride
ome, praising God for all mercies."—*The Rev. John Berridge, Vicar of Everton, and
ompanion of Wesley*.

"Your letter, my dear madam, was very acceptable. Any communications from my
ear, good Lady Huntingdon are always welcome, and always, in every particular, to
y satisfaction. I have no comfort in my own family, therefore must look for that
leasure and gratification which others can impart. I hope you will shortly come and
ee me, and give me more of your company than I have had latterly. In truth, I always
eel more happy and more contented after an hour's conversation with you than I do
fter a whole week's round of amusement. When alone, my reflections and recollections
lmost kill me, and I am forced to fly to the society of those I detest and abhor. Now
here is Lady Frances Saunderson's great rout tomorrow night—all the world will be
here, and I must go. I do hate that woman as much as I do hate a physician, but I
nust go, if for no other purpose than to mortify and spite her. This is very wicked, I
now, but I confess all my little sins to you, for I know your goodness will lead you to
e mild and forgiving, and perhaps my wicked heart may gain some good from you in
ne end.

Believe me, my dear madam, Your most faithful and most humble servant,

S. MARLBOROUGH."

—*Letter from Sarah Duchess of Marlborough to Selina, Countess of Huntingdon*.

"I thank your ladyship for the information concerning the Methodist preachers;
neir doctrines are most repulsive, and strongly tinctured with impertinence and dis-
espect towards their superiors in perpetually endeavouring to level all ranks and do

away with all distinctions. It is monstrous to be told that you have a heart as sinfu as the common wretches that crawl on the earth. This is highly offensive and insulting and I cannot but wonder that your ladyship should relish any sentiments so much a variance with high rank and good breeding. . . . .

"I have the honour to be, My dear Lady Huntingdon, Your ladyship's most faithfu and obliged, C. BUCKINGHAM."—*Letter from the Countess of Buckingham to Selina Countess of Huntingdon.*

MEDICAL AND SCIENTIFIC

"CHARLES PETER, Surgeon, Served King Charles ye 2nd in ye Dutch warrs. Surgeo of ye Horse guards to King James and Surgeon of the Household to King William daily prepares his Cordial Tincture and Pills, which have cured Thousands of ye Collick Stone, Gravell, Scurvie and Dropsey, etc. Gives advice to the Poor as well as Ric at his House in St. Martin's Lane near Long Acre, where he hath lived between thirt and forty Years. LAUS DEO 1705. ÆTAT. 57."

"LAW, DENTIST, No. 10 ST. ALBAN'S STREET, PALL MALL. Pupil of the late Mr. Rae Surgeon Dentist to His Majesty and His Royal Highness the Prince of Wales. FAMILIE attended by the Year."

CHEMISTS. "Chymical and Galenical Medicines, with all sorts of druggs. N.B. Th Elixir for the asthma as also for the Gout and Rhumatism."

"JOHN RIGG, CUPPER, At the Hummums in the Little Piazza, Covent Garden With a Back Door from Charles Street Where GENTLEMEN only May be always Ac commodated (if not full) in the best and neatest manner with LODGING, SWEATING BATHING OR CUPPING. And with the utmost Decorum as has always been kept an preserved for near an Hundred Years. LIKEWISE LADIES are permitted only to Sweating Bathing and Cupping, With great Care and Proper Attendance. N.B. Gentlemen o Ladies who desire to be Cupped at their own Houses either in Town, or Country, shal be waited on. There is likewise a good Cold Bath."—*Various Trade Cards.*

"*May* 4, 1717. A grave-digger was found taking the corpse of a man named Childer out of Bethlem churchyard, and selling the same to a surgeon, for which he was fine forty shillings, and sentenced to be whipped from Newgate to Smithfield bars."

"*Sept.* 19, 1736. The famous bone-setter of Epsom, Mrs. Mapp, continued to mak extraordinary cures, and after having set up her carriage, went to Kensington, and waite upon her Majesty."

"*March* 17, 1740. Mrs. Stephens received the £5,000 granted her by parliamen for her medicine for the cure of the stone."

—"The Universal Chronologist," II.

JOSEPH PRIESTLEY (1733-1804) became a Nonconformist minister and a great chemist He was responsible for several important advances in chemistry. He devoted himsel to the study of gases, inventing a "pneumatic trough" with which gases could b collected. He obtained hydrochloric acid gas by heating spirits of salts ; he showed b experiment that plant respiration purified vitiated air. He also discovered oxyge (1774), nitrous oxide, sulphur dioxide, and ammonia, which he decomposed electricall into nitrogen and hydrogen, and formed into sal ammoniac with hydrochloric acid. H also employed electricity to combine hydrogen and oxygen into water, though it wa Cavendish who demonstrated the result. Priestley's weakness in theory led him t cling to the absurd "phlogiston" idea : that "phlogiston" is emitted on burning ; as thi process involves an increase in weight, "phlogiston" must weigh less than nothing However, his passion for experiment led to important results, which probably le Lavoisier to find the oxygen basis of combustion.

"*Dec.* 7, 1776. A new machine was invented by Mr. Henley, for exhibiting perpetua electricity.

"Mr. Henry Cavendish made various attempts in electricity, to imitate the effec produced by the torpedo. He also published a curious account of the instruments of th Royal Society."

"*July* 11, 1778. A new lamp with 1,000 small mirrors, reflecting a very stron glare of light, was constructed by way of experiment, when it was found to be visibl much further off at sea than the Lowestoft light-house."

"*Dec.* 31, 1795. Mr. Herschel completed his celebrated telescope ; the tube of which was forty feet long, and the great mirror forty inches in diameter."

"*Nov.* 26, 1789. An account was delivered in by Mr. Herschel of the sixth and seven satellites of Saturn ; he also published a catalogue of 2,000 new stars."

"*Dec.* 12, 1794. A quintuple belt was observed by Dr. Herschel, on the planet Saturn."

"1796. The telegraph was erected over the Admiralty Office for the speed of communication of intelligence, with other similar machines placed on different heights."

"*Dec.* 28, 1798. Boulton and Watt's manufactory was lighted by gas."
"The Universal Chronologist," II.

NAVAL AND MILITARY AFFAIRS

A SIEGE ASSAULT.—One of the assailing party thus describes the critical part of the affair ; "The enemy gave us one scattering fire only, and away they ran. We jumped into the covered-way and ran after them. They made to a ravelin which covered the curtain of the fort, in which were a captain and sixty men. We, seeing them get into the ravelin, pursued them, got in with them, and soon put most of them to the sword. They that escaped us fled over a small wooden bridge, exposed to the fire of the great and small shot of the body of the fort. However, we got over the *fausse braye*, where we had nothing for it but to take the fort or die."—*Attack on Venloo, Flanders, Marlborough's Campaign, 1704 (Parker, "Military Transactions").*

PIRACY.—"*July* 11, 1723. News arrived from Jamaica that Captain Taylor, commander of a pirate vessel called the Cassandra, had made an offer to the Duke of Portland, the governor, to surrender himself and crew with most of their riches, upon condition of a pardon. That offer was refused by the duke, and he gave orders for destroying the said pirates ; upon which, Taylor proposed the same terms to the governor of Porto Bello, who immediately accepted them ; and they landed to enjoy their plunder among the Spanish Indians. It is said the value in that ship amounted to one million sterling ; one-fourth part was given to the Spanish governor, and the remainder the pirates divided among themselves, being 144 men, most of them English.

"Advices were also received from Rhode Island, that at a court of admiralty held there, twenty-five pirates taken by Captain Solgard, of the Greyhound man-of-war, had been executed on the 19th of that month."—*"The Universal Chronologist," II.*

ORDNANCE.—*Nov.* 17, 1750. "The proprietors of the new foundry at Chelsea proved one of their new invented cannons, a six-pounder, weighing only 350 pounds, on Hampstead Heath. The piece, which was fired with ball, was first charged with four pounds of powder ; the second time with five ; the third with five pounds and a half ; and the fourth with six pounds and a half. The cannon was not in the least impaired, although the quantity of powder required for an ordinary charge was only one pound and a quarter."—*"The Universal Chronologist," II.*

NAVAL AND MILITARY RATIONS.—Some idea of the food given to the soldiers in garrison may be gained by perusal of the following contract for rations (*Gazette*, September 23-27, 1712) : "The Most Honourable the Lord High Treasurer of Great Britain having receiv'd Her Majesty's Pleasure, That a Contract shall be made for Victualling Her Majesty's Garrisons at Minorca, to consist of about 4,000 Men, and at Gibraltar, to consist of about 2,000 Men, according to the Proportions underwritten for each Man for seven Days, viz :

7 Pound of Bread, or (when desir'd by the Commanders in Chief)	1 Pound of Pork
	4 Pints of Pease
A pint of Wheat instead of a Pound of Bread	3 Pints of Oatmeal
	6 Ounces of Butter
2 Pound and half of Beef	8 Ounces of Cheese

"Notwithstanding the orders provided against the buying and selling her Majesty's provisions, it is so frequently practised, even to a scandal, that in discharge of my duty I can't conceal from you an instance thereof. Yesterday a rigger was passing through the yard in my view loaded with one of her Majesty's biscuit-bags full of bread, pretending dirty bread, accompanied by a woman with a ballast-basket wherein was several pieces of meat, which, by their own confessions to me, they had bought aboard the Salisbury, and though not immediately from the purser yet was with his cognisance, as the steward told me, he seeing it go over the ship's side."—*Extract of a letter from Commander Greenhill to the Navy Board, 2nd December, 1707.*

MILITARY INCIDENTS.—"*March* 1, 1797. A battle took place at the Opera-house, between the soldiers on duty and the chairmen and footmen."

"*January* 3, 1796. Fifty soldiers were suffocated during a storm, by the hatches being closed on them in a vessel bound from Guernsey to Cowes."

"*May* 4, 1795. Fourteen men perished in the *Boyne*, man-of-war, which vessel, having caught fire, blew up at Spithead."

"*May* 17, The Oxfordshire militia, on a seizure of flour at Newhaven, committed a riot."

June 1. Two of the Oxfordshire militia were shot for riots at Newhaven."—*"The Universal Chronologist," II.*

THE PRESS GANG.—Moritz notes in his "Travels" (1782), the English system of pressing for the navy. "There is nothing for the foreigner to fear," he writes, "unless he be found in a suspicious place. A singular invention for this purpose of pressing is a vessel placed on Tower Hill, furnished with masts and all the appurtenances of a ship. The persons attending this ship promise simple country people who happen to be standing staring at it, to show it to them for a trifle ; and, as soon as they are in, they are secured as in a trap ; and, according to circumstances, made sailors of, or let go again."

"*June* 2, 1741. This day commenced the hottest press below bridge which had been known since the commencement of the Spanish war. All seamen were seized, whether they had protections or not, so that in 36 hours the number enrolled on the navy books amounted to 2,370 hands."

"*April* 10, 1791. The lieutenant of a press-gang was fined forty shillings, for forcibly entering a house."—*"The Universal Chronologist," II.*

HISTORICAL CHART, 1700-1800

Year	Rulers of England and France	Other Important European Rulers	Important Events	Some Well-Known People (Named in order of date of birth)	Principal Buildings
1700	William III Louis XIV	. . . . .	. . . . .	John Churchill, Duke of Marlborough, English general (1650-1722)	Greenwich Hospital (N. Hawksmoor) 1696-1715
1702	Anne	. . . . .	. . . . .	Daniel Defoe, English author (c. 1659-1731)	Castle Howard (Sir J. Vanbrugh), 1702-1714
1704	. . . . .	. . . . .	Capture of Gibraltar .	Jonathan Swift, English author (1667-1745)	Easton Neston, Northants (N. Hawksmoor) 1713
				Joseph Addison, English essayist (1672-1719)	St. Mary, Woolmoth (N. Hawksmoor) 1713-1719
1707	. . . . .	. . . . .	Act of Union between England and Scotland .	Sir Robert Walpole, English Prime Minister (1676-1745)	St. George's, Hanover Sq. (J. James) 1720
				Johann Sebastian Bach, German composer (1685-1750)	Stoneleigh Abbey, Kenilworth(Smith of Warwick) c. 1720
1709	. . . . .	. . . . .	Battle of Malplaquet .	George Frederick Handel, German composer (1685-1759)	Moor Park (G. Leoni), 1720
				John Gay, English poet (1685-1732)	St. Martin's-in-the-Field (J. Gibbs), 1721-1726
				Alexander Pope, English poet (1688-1744)	Admiralty Buildings (T. Ripley), 1722-1726
1713	. . . . .	Philip V of Spain and Frederick William I of Prussia .	Peace of Utrecht	Samuel Richardson, English novelist (1689-1761)	Houghton, Norfolk (C. Campbell, T. Ripley, W. Kent), 1723
1714	George I			James Oglethorpe, English general and philanthropist (1696-1785)	Christ Church, Spitalfields (N. Hawksmoor), 1725
1715	Louis XV	. . . .	. . . . .	William Pitt, Earl of Chatham, English statesman (1708-1778)	Villa at Chiswick (Earl of Burlington), 1729
1718	. . . . .	Death of Charles XII of Sweden .	. . . . .	Samuel Johnson, English writer (1709-1784)	Queen's Sq., Bath (Wood of Bath), c. 1730
1720	. . . . .		South Sea Bubble	Dr. Arne, English composer (1710-1778)	Nostell Priory (J. Paine), 1735-1751
				Lawrence Sterne, English writer (1713-1768)	Radcliffe Library, Oxford (J. Gibbs), 1737-1747
1725	. . . . .	Death of Peter the Great of Russia	. . . . .	David Garrick, English actor (1717-1779)	Wentworth Wood House, Yorks (H. Flitcroft), 1740
1727	George II			Thomas Chippendale, English cabinet-maker (c. 1718-1779)	Mansion House, London (Dance, the Elder), c. 1740
				Sir Joshua Reynolds, English painter (1723-1792)	
				Robert Clive, English statesman (1725-1774)	Doncaster Mansion House (J. Paine), 1745-1748
				John Howard, English prison reformer (1726-1790)	Woburn Abbey (H. Flitcroft) 1747
				James Wolfe, English general (1727-1759)	Chesterfield House (I. Ware), 1747-1752
				Thomas Gainsborough, English painter (1727-1788)	Prior Park, Bath (Wood of Bath), c. 1750
1740	. . . . .	Frederick the Great of Prussia .	Outbreak of War of Austrian Succession .	Oliver Goldsmith, British poet, novelist and playwright (1728-1774)	Horse Guards (W. Kent), 1753
1745	. . . . .	. . . . .	Jacobite Rebellion	Robert Adam, British architect (with his brothers) (1728-1792)	Holkham, Norfolk (M. Brettingham and W. Kent), c. 1754
1750	. . . . .	. . . . .	. . . . .	Edmund Burke, British statesman and political writer (1729-1797)	University Library, Cambridge (S. Wright), 1754-1758
1756	. . . . .	. . . . .	Outbreak of Seven Years' War .	Josiah Wedgwood, English manufacturer of pottery (1730-1795)	Town Hall, Blandford (Bastard), 1754
1757	. . . . .	. . . . .	Battle of Plassey	George Washington, first President, U.S.A. (1732-1799)	White's Club, (R. Adam), c. 1755
1759	. . . . .	. . . . .	Capture of Quebec	Warren Hastings, English statesman, first governor-general of British India (1732-1818)	Harewood House, Yorks (Carr, and R. Adam),1760
1760	George III				Fitzroy Square, London (R. Adam), c. 1760
1762	. . . . .	Catherine II of Russia .	. . . . .	Sir Richard Arkwright, English inventor (1732-1792)	Bowood, Wilts (Dance, the Younger), 1760 and later
1763	. . . . .		Peace of Paris	George Romney, English painter (1734-1802)	Kedleston (J. Paine and R. Adam), 1761
				Edward Gibbon, English historian (1737-1794)	Spencer House, Green Park (J. Vardy), 1762
				Charles James Fox, British statesman and orator (1737-1794)	Lansdowne House (R. Adam), c. 1765
				Richard Brinsley Sheridan, British playwright (1751-1816)	The Adelphi (R. Adam), 1768 and later
1774	Louis XVI	. . . .	. . . . .	Thomas Sheraton, English furniture-designer and cabinet-maker (c. 1751-1806)	Assembly Rooms, Bath (Wood, the Younger), 1769-1771
1775			Battles of Lexington and Bunker's Hill		Newgate Prison (G. Dance the Younger), 1770
1776	. . . . .	. . . . .	Establishment of United States .	Samuel Crompton, English inventor (1753-1827)	Sir W. Wynne's House, 20 St. James's Square (R. Adam), 1771-1774
				John Flaxman, English sculptor (1755-1826)	Ely House, Dover Street (Sir R. Taylor), c. 1772
1783	. . . . .		Treaty of Versailles	Wolfgang Mozart, Austrian composer (1756-1791)	Somerset House (Sir W. Chambers), 1776-1786
				Horatio Nelson, British admiral (1758-1805)	Finsbury Square, London (Dance, the Younger) 1777-1791
1789	. . . . .	. . . . .	Outbreak of French Revolution	William Wilberforce, English philanthropist (1759-1833)	
1792	. . . . .	. . . . .	Outbreak of 1st Napoleonic War	William Pitt the Younger, English statesman (1758-1806)	Greenwich Chapel Interior (J. Stuart), 1774
1793	. . . . .	. . . . .	Execution of Louis XVI .	Arthur Wellesley, Duke of Wellington, English general and statesman (1769-1852)	Richmond Bridge (J. Paine) 1780-1783
1798	. . . . .	. . . . .	Battle of the Nile	Ludwig van Beethoven, German composer (1770-1827)	Custom House, and Four Courts, Dublin (J. Gandon), 1781-1800
1800	. . . . .	. . . . .	. . . . .	Napoleon Bonaparte, Emperor of France (1769-1821)	Pump Room, Bath (T. Baldwin), 1795

The first bars of two typical 18th Century songs. From "Clio and Euterpe"
a contemporary collection.

PLATE 4

(a) A chamber concert; a lady conducting; another strikes the zither with two curved sticks. (b) The Chevalier d'Eon, in a panier-dress. (c) A *tête-à-tete* by the window. (d) Polite society strolling at Ranelagh. (e) An assembly at the Pantheon. [All Anon. eng., pubrs. possn.]

PLATE 5

(a)

(b)

(c)

(d)

(a) Two ladies in animated gossip. (b) The engagement is announced. [(a) and (b)
V. & A. M. Print Room, Portf. 0 2 d.] (c) Lady Dundas presenting colours to the
Royal East Indian Volunteers. [From Griggs' " Relics of the Hon. E. India Co.,"
1790.] (d) Actor in a play called " The Rehearsal." [Skelton eng. after p. by Graham
in the V. & A. Mus., S. Kens.]

PLATE 6

(a)

(b)

(c)

(a) Around the tea-table in the garden at Wilton Ho. Wilts., ca. 1750; note the little black servant. [Luke Sullivan eng.] (b) Three garden groves at the Earl of Burlington's villa, Chiswick, ca. 1750. [Anon. eng.; pubrs. possn.] (c) Showing the vicar the garden—a scene from the novel " Pamela " by Richardson, ca. 1750. [Eng. from a painting by Joseph Highmore.]

PLATE 7

(a)

(b)

(a) Descending from a coach at the mansion steps, Stowe, 1739. (b) Sailing my lord's barge on the lake, Stowe, 1739. [(a) and (b) Jean Rigaud: " Illustrations of Stowe House, Bucks."]

PLATE 8

(a)

(b)

(c)

(a) Opening of the Radcliffe Library, Oxford, 1751. [Oxford Almanack—
G. Vertue eng.] (b) and (c) Two views of a Thanksgiving Service at
St. Paul's for the recovery of George III in 1784. [E. Dayes eng.]

PLATE 9

(b)

(a)

(a) A view of the House of Commons, ca. 1750. [B. Cole eng.] (b) A Lord Mayor's Banquet at the Mansion House, ca. 1770. [Eng. in Guildhall Library.]

PLATE 10

(c)

(b)

(e)

(a)

(d)

(a) Selling ballads outside the Fleet Prison; note long wig and child with doll. [Eng. in Guildhall Libry.] (b) Execution of 11 people at Newgate, including several women, 1783. [Anon. eng.] (c) The arrest. [Eng. after Thomas Stothard, R.A.] (d) The exercise yard at the Fleet Prison; skittles and a kind of racquets, ca. 1800. [Pugin and Rowlandson eng.] (e) Jonathan Wild carted through the streets, 1725. [Anon. eng., V. & A. M. Print Room.]

PLATE 11

The first day of term, Westminster Hall. Lawyers' consultations, print and bookstalls, etc. [Gravelot dr., C. Mosley eng. repub. 1797.]

PLATE 12

(a)

(b)

(a) Horse-racing at Ascot, 1792. [J. N. Sartorius dr., J. Eady eng.] (b) The hunt
moving off, 1790. [Eng. after pntg. by J. N. Sartorius.]

PLATE 13

(a)

(b)

(c)

(a) " Four Corners " played at the Swan, Chelsea, ca. 1730. [Pub. by Carington Bowles.] (b) The ladies' cricket match. T. H. ex. 1779. [Anon. pntg. M.C.C. Colln., Lord's Cricket Gnd.] (c) Cricket; ca. 1750. [Eng. after Francis Hayman.]
[Both (b) and (c) show the early two-stump wicket and curved bat—note that in (c) the scorer sits notching.]

PLATE 14

(b)

(a)

(d)

(c)

(a) A game of billiards, 1752. [Trade-card of E. Turpin, candlemaker.] (b) Partridge-shooting with a spaniel, 1777. [From George Edie: "The Art of Shooting."] (c) A game of battledore, ca. 1750. [Eng. after Francis Haynan.] (d) The Allemande Dance, ca. 1765. [C. Grignion eng.]

(d)

(e)

(f)

(a) The old gentleman practises fencing on wall-figures, ca. 1750. [F. Hayman dr., C. Grignion, eng.] (b) The game of Hide-the handkerchief." [Lancret p.; Boitard eng.] (c) The last card takes the trick. [Bodl. Liby. Douce Prints, E 21.] (d) The peep-show, ca. 1700. [Anon. eng.] (e) A chamber concert, ca. 1780. [Anon eng.; pubrs. possn.] (f) Backgammon, ca. 1760. [A. Walker eng.]

61

PLATE 16

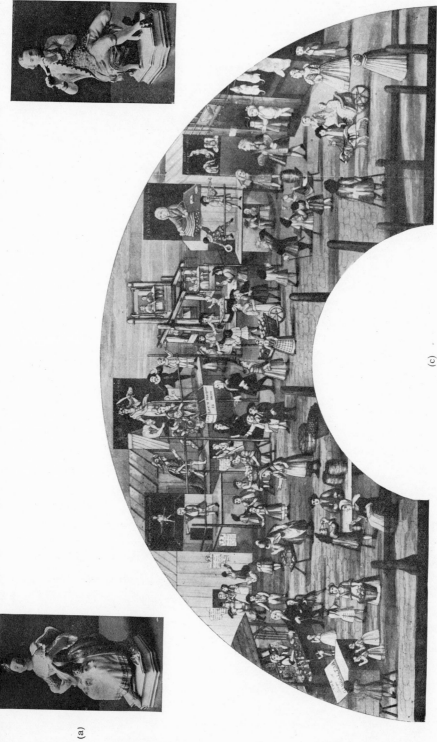

(a) and (b) Playing the guitar and flute. [Two china figures in the V. & A. Mus., S. Kens.] (c) Bartholomew Fair at Smithfield in 1721. Showing peepshow, toy-stall, tightrope walker, conjurors, acrobats, food-stalls, etc. From an engraving after a drawing on a fan. [B. M Crace Colln.]

PLATE 17

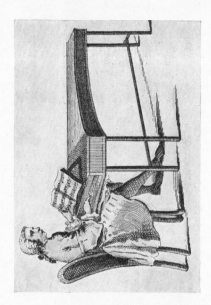

(a)

(b)

(d)

(c)

(a) An open-air concert, 1739. [J. Rigaud, " Illustrations of Stowe."] (b) Practising on the harpsichord. [Anon eng., B. M.] (c) street musicians make a hideous din outside a deaf asylum, ca. 1755. [J. Collet dr.] (d) A street concert party in Grosvenor Square, ca. 1770. [E. Dayes eng.]

PLATE 18

(a)

(b)

(a) A theatre scene; the play, " The Street of London," 1774. [J. F. Delsing, " De Niewe Schonburg de Amsterdam."] (b) A scene from Gay's " Beggar's Opera," first produced in 1728. [W. Hogarth eng.]

PLATE 19

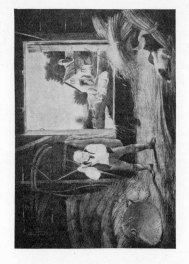

(c)

(d)

(a)

(b)

(a) Ploughing with a four-horse team, ca. 1803. [W. H. Pyne eng.]   (b) Haymaking in Highbury Fields, ca. 1780. [Anon. eng.; pubrs. possn.]
(c) The old thresher at work in the barn, 1800. [Painted by R. Westall, R.A., W. S. Reynolds eng.]   (d) A haymaking dance. [Painted on a jug at the
V. & A. Mus., S. Kens.]

PLATE 20

(b)

(c)

(a) In the dairy. [Anon. eng. V. & A. M. Print Room, Portf. 0 2 C.] (b) The farmer and his workers, 1793. [Anon. eng., B. M. Print Room 36 H 10.] (c) Beating pans to take the swarm of bees. [Anon. eng. of Seasons :—Oct. Bodl. Liby. Douce Prints Portf. 137.]

PLATE 21

(c)

(b)

(a)

(a) A general view of country occupations : milking, churns, well, haycarts, mills, etc., c. 1727. [Richard Bradley, " The Country Ladies' Director."]
(b) Gardening at a country house, with glass cultivation, 1793. [John Evelyn, " The Compleat Gardener."] (c) Field-work, 1727. [Richard Bradley, " The Country Gentleman and Farmer's Monthly Director."]

PLATE 22

(a)

(b)

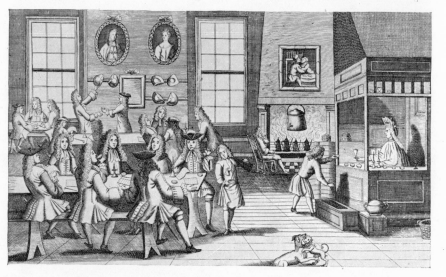

(c)

(a) A scene outside Drury Lane Theatre, 1776. [R. and J. Adam's " Works in Architecture," 3 vols.] (b) John Lofting's fire-engines at work, ca. 1720. [Contemporary prospectus. B. M. Crace Colln.] (c) A typical coffee-house interior, ca. 1740. [Bodl. Liby. Douce Prints W 1.2]

PLATE 23

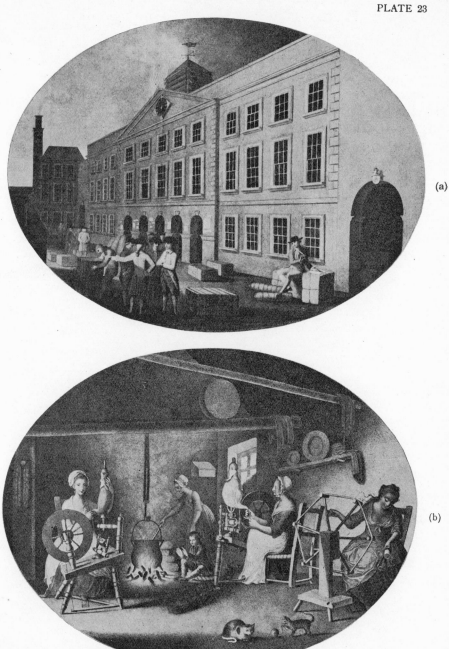

(a)

(b)

(a) Linen packed for export outside the Linen Hall, Dublin, 1791. (b) Spinning, boiling the yarn, reeling with the clock reel at home, 1791. [(a) and (b) W. Hincks. "Illustrations of the Irish Linen Industry."]

The Stocks-market, on the site of the present Mansion House, 1738; St. Stephen's Walbrook in the background. The statue is of Sobieski, King of Poland, trampling on the Turk, altered to represent Charles II treading down Cromwell. [Jos. Nichols dr., H. Fletcher eng.]

79

PLATE 25

(c)

(b)

(d)

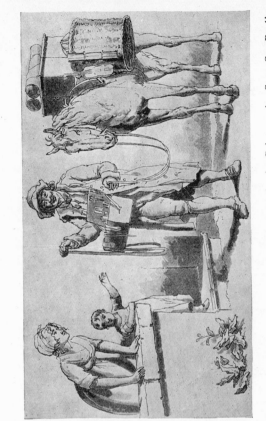

(a)

(a) An arcade of shops, ca. 1773. [Anon, eng.] (b) A visit to the linen drapers, ca. 1720. [Trade-card of Benjamin Cole, at the Sun, St. Paul's Churchyard. B. Cole eng.] (c) Masefield's wall-paper warehouse in the Strand, ca. 1750. [Contemporary Trade-card.] (d) The Pedlar's visit, ca. 1803. [W. H. Pyne eng.]

(e)

(d)

(a)

(a) The blacksmith's forge, ca. 1780. [Jos. Wright of Derby p.; R. Earlom eng.] (b) The water-carrier. (c) The knife-grinder, 1711. [(b) and (c) Tempest's " Cries of London."] (d) The shoeing-forge, ca, 1790. (e) Pillow lace-makers, ca. 1790. [(d) and (e) Thos. Rowlandson eng.]

83

PLATE 21

(b)

(d)

(a)

(c)

(a) Transporting stone in the masons' yard. (b) The wheelwright at work. (c) Weighing and carting stone. (d) The butcher delivers the joint. All ca. 1803. [W. H. Pyne eng.]

(b)

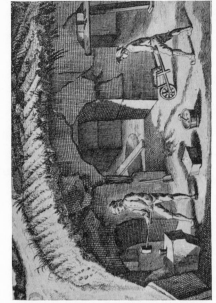

(d)

(a)

(c)

(a) The Throwster's Mill winding thread from skeins into bobbins. The girl waits to join breaking threads, ca. 1759. (b) The currier workshop, ca. 1759. [(a) and (b) "A New Univ. Hist. of Arts and Sciences."]   (c) Dyeing tapestry in vats, ca. 1760. (d) Quarrying underground. [(c) and (d) Diderot, "Encyclopædia."]

PLATE 29

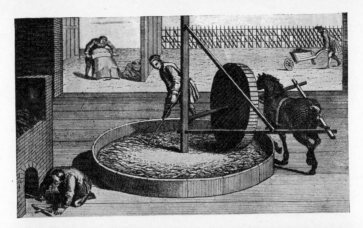

(a)

(b)

(c)

(a) A horse-driven grinding mill in a tanner's workshop. c. 1759.
[S. Marenia dr.] (b) Glass-blowing. c. 1759. (c) Spinning and weaving,
with a girl to refill shuttles. Before the use of Kay's flying
shuttles, c. 1759. [S. Marenia dr.] [(a), (b) and (c) " A New Univ.
Hist. of Arts and Sciences."]

PLATE 30

(a)

(b)

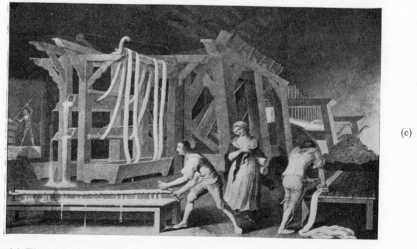

(c)

(a) The barber and wig-maker's shop, ca. 1765. [Diderot, " Encyclopædia."]
(b) Linen manufacture : winding, warping, weaving with shuttle filler as
usual, 1791. (c) A bleach-mill, showing washmill, rubbing boards and beetling
engine, 1791. [(b) and (c) from W. Hincks, " Illustr. of Irish Linen Industry."

PLATE 31

(c)

(d)

(b)

(e)

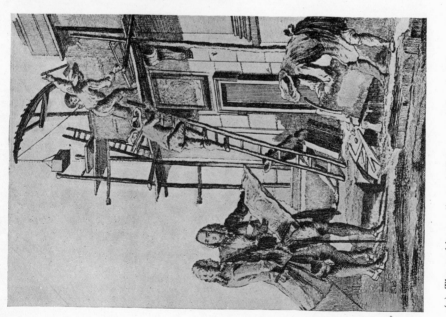

(a)

(a) The architects direct building operations. [From a French edition of Vignola's "Five Orders," 1767. Cochin and Charpentier eng.]
(b) The building owner's visit, ca. 1730. [Anon. eng., pub. by Robert Sayer.] (c) Stone working. (d) Wall building. [(c) and (d) Pozzo's Perspective, 1707.] (e) Roofing with pantiles at Southgate, Yarmouth, ca. 1800. [Anon. eng., pub. R. Wilkinson.]

93

(a) A five-horse wagon going through London, ca. 1720. [J. Kip eng.] (b) The carter takes sheep in his horse's paniers, Walton, Surrey, 1751. [Luke Sullivan eng.] (c) The road-menders, 1790. [Eng. after George Stubbes, R.A., p.] (d) Linen workers outside the Brown Linen Market, Banbridge, Co. Down, Ireland, 1791. [W. Hincks: " Illus. of Irish Linen Industry."]

PLATE 33

(a)

(b)

(c)

(a) A sedan-chair stand in Whitehall, 1724. [J. Kip eng.] (b) A coach stand outside Montague House, London. ca. 1720. [Sutton Nicholls eng.] (c) Pamela in her coach, ca. 1750. [Eng. after Joseph Highmore.]

PLATE 34

(a)

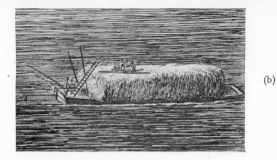

(b)

(c)

(d)

(e)

(a) The barge at London Bridge, 1775. [W. Harrison : " Description of London and Westminster."]   (b) A hay-barge on the Thames, 1720. [J. Kip eng.] (c) Ferrying a coach and pair at Chelsea, 1720. [J. Kip. eng.] (d) A sailing barge drawn by four horses, ca. 1790. [T. Rowlandson eng.] (e) Smugglers loading their pack-train, ca. 1803. [W. H. Pyne eng.]

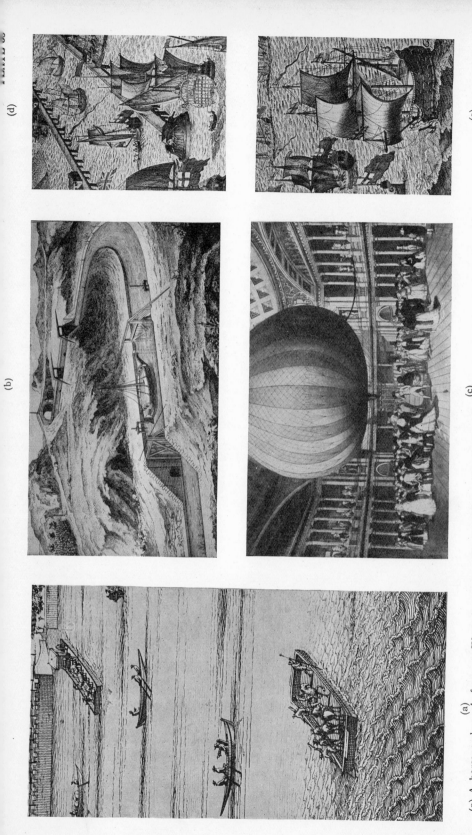

(a) A horse and coach ferry at Westminster, ca. 1720. [J. Kip eng.] (b) A barge passing through a chain of locks on a canal, ca. 1770. [Diderot, " Encyclopaedia."] (c) Lunardi's Balloon at the Pantheon, Oxford St., ca. 1785. [G. Byrom eng.] (d) and (e) Ships near Dunkirk Harbour, ca. 1720. [J. Kip eng.]

(b)

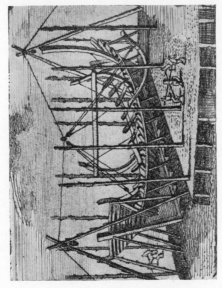

(d)

(a)

(c)

(a) The launch of a King's ship, ca. 1725. (b) A ship careened for under-water repairs at Sheerness, ca. 1725. (c) a first-rate battleship firing; sails clewed up, 1721. (d) On the stocks: constructing a ship's rib at Deptford, ca. 1725. [(a), (b) and (d) T. Miller dr.; P. C. Canot eng.]

103

PLATE 37

(a)

(b)

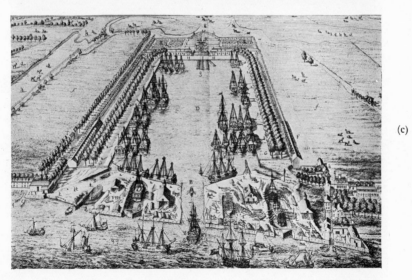

(c)

(a) The second Custom House, London, c. 1720. [G. Toms eng.] (b) Landing French people and goods at the old Custom House by the Tower, 1757. A satire on imports. [S. P. Boitard, dr. and eng.] (c) Howland Great Dock, Deptford, ca. 1720. [T. Badeslade eng.]

PLATE 38

(a)

(b)

(c)

(a) Whalers at work, 1721. (b) The " Royal Sovereign," 1721. [(a) and
(b) T. Baston eng.] (c) Warships in Plymouth Sound, ca. 1720. [J. Kip eng.]

(c)

(d)

(a) Interior of a Georgian church, with parson and clerk. [Eng. pub. T. Bowles. V. & A. M. Print Rm., Portf. 0 5 a.] (b) Pamela's quiet wedding, ca. 1750. [Eng. after J. Highmore.] (c) Burial within the church; opening the vault. [Eng. after T. Stothard, R.A.] (d) Whitefield preaching at Moorfields, 1750. [R. Prancker eng.]

109

PLATE 40

(a)

(b)

(c)

(a) The parson's school, ca. 1750. [S. Wale dr.; Walker eng.] (b) New arrivals at the Dame School. [Anon. eng., V. & A. M. Print Rm., Portf. 0 3 E.] (c) Salvador House Academy for Boys, Tooting, 1787. [J. Walker dr. and eng.]

PLATE 41

(a)

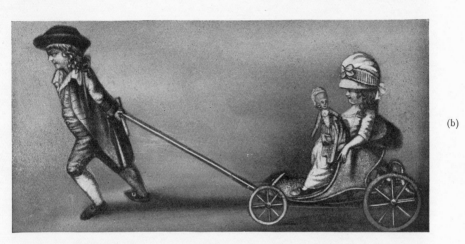

(b)

(c)

(a) Boys bowling hoops in the streets of Oxford, 1781. [Oxford Almanack, M. A. Rooker, dr. and eng.] (b) Children with go-cart and doll, at Bagnigge Wells, ca. 1780. [Eng. pub. by Carington Bowles.] (c) Pamela among her children and servants, ca. 1750. [Eng. after p. by Joseph Highmore.]

PLATE 42

(a)

(b)

(c)

(d)

(a) Drawing from the model, ca. 1770. [Aquatint eng. after Jos. Wright of Derby.]
(b) A Dublin promenade, St. Stephen's Green, ca. 1790. [T. Malton dr. and eng.]
(c) The Art School, ca. 1755 (Diderot, " Encyclopædia.") (d) Trinity Coll. Library.
Dublin, ca. 1790. [T. Malton dr. and eng.]

PLATE 42

(b)

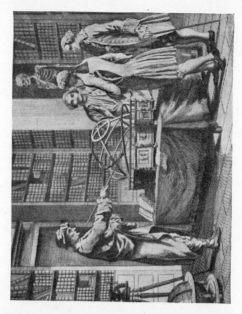

(c)

(a)

(a) Charles Towneley and connoisseur friends among his collection of marbles at Queen Anne's Gate. (Much of it is now in the Brit. Mus.) [Eng. after the picture by J. Zoffany, R.A.] (b) Chemical experiments, ca. 1740. [Anon. eng., V. & A. M. Print Rm., Costume Section.] (c) Demonstrating an astronomical model, ca. 1760. [S. Wale dr.; B. Cole eng.]

PLATE 44

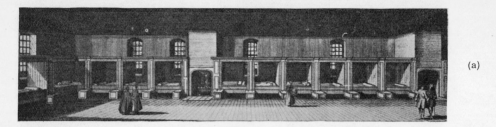

(a)

(b)

(c)

(d)

(a) A ward at Guy's Hospital, 1725. [Eng. pub. by Bowles.] (b) A men's hospital, ca. 1740. [Mettenleiter, eng.] (c) The lady has the vapours; the doctor seems concerned. [Chodowiecki dr.; Geyser eng.] (d) Casting the dead into a plague pit, ca. 1700. (Note smoking as a precaution.) [Anon. eng., V. & A. M. Print Rm.]

PLATE 45

(a) "Present; fire!" (b) "Join your right hand to your firelock," ca. 1730. [From "Gentlemen Associators of London and Westminster."] (c) The duel begins, ca. 1750. (d) A duel ends with a bad chest wound, ca. 1750. [(c) and (d) S. Wale dr.; C. Grignion eng.] (e) and (f) Camp scenes in Marlborough's campaigns, ca. 1710. [(e) playing dice on a drum; (f) cooking and cards. Paul Decker eng.]

PLATE 46

(a)

(b)

(a) Relief of the Siege of Gibraltar by Admiral Leake, 1705. British ships in actions with Spanish. [Paul Decker dr. and eng.] (b) Bridport's action with the French off Port L'Orient, June 23, 1795. The Tigre just surrendering to the flagship Royal George. [T. Whitcombe p.; Bailey eng.]

123

PLATE 47

(a)

(b)

(c)

(a) A convoy of army waggons. (b) Guns in action. (c) In the gun emplacements during a bombardment of a besieged city. [(a), (b) and (c) B. Cole eng.]

26 4/3

70